# LAUREL and HARDY
## The European Tours

by

## "A.J" Marriot

Marriot Publishing

**LAUREL and HARDY – The European Tours**
First published November 2014
3rd print July 2019
Marriot Publishing
Text Copyright © by "A.J" Marriot 2014
Printed by "lulu.com"

Written, compiled, and designed by "A.J" Marriot. Layout by "A.J" Marriot
"Travelling trunk" COVER DESIGN by "A.J" Marriot
Cover artwork by Paul Wood (TT Litho, Rochester, Kent. ME2 4LX ) — www.ttlitho.co.uk

ISBN 978-0-9521308-7-1

# PREFACE

### by author "A.J" Marriot

This book, as a story, is not complete, and never could be – for the simple reason that I wasn't *there*, and the people who *were* there, aren't *here*. It is meant only to supply details of the theatres at which Laurel and Hardy played; the hotels at which they stayed; the acts with whom they worked; the people they met, the functions they attended; their modes of transport; and the impact they made on the public, both off-stage and on, during the European Tours.

Between 1987 and 1993, when I was researching and writing my first book – *LAUREL & HARDY – The British Tours* – I had the advantage of personal accounts from hundreds of people who had met, worked with, or served the two comedians in some way. However, more than two decades on, there aren't so many eye-witnesses around. Of the few who are, locating them is a major task as, in this instance, they are scattered throughout all the European countries Laurel and Hardy visited. Even after tracking down anyone with information to offer, there is still the language barrier to overcome.

So once again, as with my "British Tours" and "US Tours" books, newspapers have been invaluable in providing reliable dates, along with interesting comments and reviews, from the time. Personal accounts often become embellished or distorted over the years, whereas the contemporary viewpoints in newspapers remain unaltered – hence the prominence of quotations from this medium, within this book. In most cases, those articles thought to contain inaccuracies or fabrication have been commented upon and corrected, where possible. Many others were of such poor content, that they were deemed not worthy of being repeated.

Having stated the reason for the extensive usage of newspaper reports, I am delighted to say that, thanks to some of my European friends and fellow-researchers, this account of the European Tours has been greatly added to — firstly by extracts from some of the eye-witnesses, conducted many years ago; along with other findings such as documents, news clips, and photographs. My gratitude to them is further acknowledged in the aptly name "Acknowledgments."

Because of the number of countries visited, and the different languages therein, every single snippet of information had to be translated into English. My own "schoolboy" French and Spanish helped, to a point, but this book would have contained nothing but nonsense had it not been for some painstaking attention by a group of dedicated European friends in translating the vast number of newspaper write-ups and reviews – namely Chris James and Bibbi Johansson (Swedish); Peter Mikkelsen (Danish); Marc de Coninck (French); Benedetto Gemma (Italian); and Bram Reijnhoudt (Dutch). A tip of the hat also must go to 'Google translator,' which got the text somewhat closer, before the linguists moved in to sort out the syntax, idioms, and colloquialisms. Should a need rise up inside you to criticise any errors within the English text, please consider the enormity of the task. Because not everything translates perfectly into English, the language of origin of many newspaper write-ups has been included, to aid those for whom English is a second language. Any mistakes are purely the responsibility of the author.

Someone once said: "It is the duty of a writer to tell people something they didn't already know."

I trust I have done my duty.

### *"A.J" Marriot*

Bouquets to the author at ajmarriot@aol.com (but not too many brickbats, please! I'm sensitive.) Corrections will be better received, and additions and amendments gratefully so.

I hope you get as much fun out of reading it, as I got out of researching it.

# ACKNOWLEDGEMENTS

Four people who could have solved the great untold mysteries of the European tours – Stan and Ida Laurel, and Oliver and Lucille Hardy – were sadly departed from this world, long before my research began. How lucky I was, therefore, that five researchers, from five different countries stepped in, and very generously shared everything they had on the subject.

My heartfelt thanks and friendship go out, firstly, to Benedetto Gemma — Grand Sheik of the Laurel and Hardy Tent *"Noi Siamo le Colonne"* (*A Chump at Oxford*) (Italy) — who could have written his own book on "Laurel and Hardy in Italy," but made the extremely generous gesture of passing on all of his research to me. Likewise was Chris James — an Englishman now domiciled in Sweden, and top researcher — who went to extreme lengths to gather every piece of the puzzle making up the picture of "Laurel and Hardy in Sweden."

Third was Bram Reijnhoudt — editor and publisher of the Laurel and Hardy fanzine *Blotto* (Netherlands) — who passed on material he had acquired over a thirty-year period. Fourth is Peter Mikkelsen – who works for the Danish Film Institute — and who unselfishly shared information and photos, even though he had his own writing project on the subject of "Laurel and Hardy in Denmark."

And then there is Marc DeConinck — Grand Sheik of the *"Me and My Pal Tent"* (Belgium) — who took it upon himself to visit libraries and spend days tracking down contemporary newspaper reports on Stan and Ollie's various theatre dates, throughout Belgium.

These five then extended their assistance even further, by translating every piece of text they had, from its language of origin, into English. Dedication like that is so hard to find, and I cannot thank them enough. Without their considerable assistance, this book would have told only a fraction of the full story.

Others who gave valued assistance, by donating text and/or photographs, are:

DENMARK: Torben Moeller (Grand Sheik of the 'Be Big' Tent); Flemming Nielsen; Ulla Nymand. GERMANY: Michael Ehret; Harry Hoppe; Gunther Mathias. NETHERLANDS: Siep Bousma; Sjaak Bolder; John Den Heijer. USA: Paul E. Gierucki; Bernie Hogya; Paul Hasse. SWEDEN: Bibbi Johansson (Picture Editor (*Aftonbladet*). ENGLAND: Steve Robinson; and David Wyatt – who generously shared his notes on Newsreel footage.

ITALY: Antonio Costa Barbé (interviews with Sordi and Zambuto); Andrea Benfante (research on Genova); Andrea Ciaffaroni (research on Rome); Enzo Pio Pignatiello (research on archives, and Vatican); Alessandro Rossini (research on San Remo); Alessandro Santi (Grand Sheik of *"Block-Heads"*, Italy); Giancarlo Manfredini; and Annamaria Moreschi. All of them have my utmost thanks.

And finally to Rob Lewis (Grand Sheik of the 'Helpmates UK' Tent) for his contribution, assistance and support in so many ways.

-------0---------

## BIBLIOGRAPHY

"ATOLL K – The Final Film of Laurel and Hardy," Norbert Aping (McFarland)

-----0-----

## IMAGE SOURCES

Archivo Moreschi – TopFoto – The Danish Film Institute – Carlsberg
Google images – Getty/Corbis/Keystone Images – Rex Features – Author's Collection

www.fotozwarthoed.com

It isn't that long ago when the only way to receive photographs was by negatives or prints being sent by post. Nowadays, with email, and especially with tens of thousands of images available to download from the Internet, keeping tabs on the source of photographs is nigh on impossible. My sincerest apologies, therefore, to anyone I may have omitted to acknowledge as source.

# CONTENTS

| | | | |
|---|---|---|---|
| TITLE PAGE | | | i |
| COPYRIGHT ISBN | | | ii |
| PREFACE | | | iii |
| ACKNOWLEDGEMENTS | | | iv |
| CONTENTS | | | v |
| Picture — Lido de Paris | | | vi |
| Chapter 1 | **THE 1947 BRITISH TOUR** | Britain 1947 | 1 |
| Chapter 2 | **A EUROPEAN DRIVING LICENCE** | Denmark 1947 | 7 |
| Chapter 3 | **KEEP STATIONERY** | Sweden 1947 pt1 | 16 |
| Chapter 4 | **SWEDEN SOUR** | Sweden 1947 pt2 | 23 |
| Chapter 5 | **THE ROYAL COUPLE** | Denmark pt2 | 31 |
| Chapter 6 | **KING AND COMEDY** | France 1947 pt1 | 35 |
| Chapter 7 | **REVUE AND REVIEWS** | France pt2 | 42 |
| Chapter 8 | **THE THEATRE OF DREAMS** | Belgium 1947 pt1 | 48 |
| Chapter 9 | **IT'S SHOWTIME!** | Belgium pt2 | 57 |
| Chapter 10 | **ON THE WRONG TRACK** | Belgium 1948 pt3 | 63 |
| Chapter 11 | **ONE NIGHTERS** | Belgium pt4 | 71 |
| Chapter 12 | **A FRENCH FARCE** | France 1950 pt1 | 78 |
| Chapter 13 | **STATION TO STATION** | Italy 1950 pt1 | 85 |
| Chapter 14 | **THROWN TO THE LIONS** | Italy pt2 | 92 |
| Chapter 15 | **NOT ATOLL WELL** | France 1950-51 pt2 | 98 |
| Chapter 16 | **BACK IN THE USA** | UK and US 1952-56 | 106 |
| Gallery | **LAUREL and HARDY in FUNLAND** | Europe 1947-51 | 111 |
| The Author | Further reading | | 121 |

-o-o-o-0-o-o-o-

## KEY

(*ibid*) = previously mentioned

(*circa*) = around this time

(*sic*) = copied correctly from original

[Square brackets] = author's comments.

Laurel **&** Hardy = on-screen – Laurel **and** Hardy = off-screen

Stan Laurel (formerly Arthur Stanley Jefferson. aka: Stanley)

Oliver Norvell Hardy (aka: "Babe" Hardy, and "Ollie")

What do mean, "*I have nothing to say*"?

CHAPTER 1

## THE 1947 BRITISH TOUR

The end of Laurel and Hardy's film career pretty much coincided with the end of World War II. Between 1941 and 1945 they had made films with Twentieth Century Fox *and* MGM, but it had not been a happy time for them, and there was no way they would work for either company again. In 1940 they had adapted to performing 'live on stage' and, in that year, and between filming in 1941 and 42, made three major city-to-city tours in the USA, plus played troop shows on and around militarised islands in the Caribbean.

[AJM: See my book: *LAUREL and HARDY – The US Tours.*]

Acting *as* soldiers, on screen.　　　　　　Acting *to* soldiers, in front of a screen.

*Great Guns* – 20th Century Fox (1941)　　　　St. Croix (Caribbean tour) – 3rd November 1941

Now in 1945, with filming a closed door; visiting Army bases being too uncomfortable, too exhausting, and not exactly what one could term a future; and vaudeville and night clubs not exactly the right medium for their soft-approach humour; the former screen stars were in real danger of never working again. It would be twenty months before they did work, when a life-line appeared from an unexpected source, in an unexpected medium:

Over in England a young theatrical entrepreneur, Bernard Delfont, was starting to make a name for himself as a booker of Variety shows. Taking advantage of the sailing de-restrictions across the Atlantic, he thought to establish his name on the map by placing it alongside that of "Laurel & Hardy." Delfont's first idea had been to invite them over to play in pantomime; but, when Laurel informed him about the three successful stage tours of North America they had done – playing *The Driver's Licence* sketch – he changed his *modus operandi* and booked them on a provisional twelve-week engagement of British variety theatres.

Leaving Los Angeles on 31st January 1947, Laurel and Hardy, made the three-to-four-day, trans-America train journey to New York where, on 5th February, after a one or two night hotel stay, they boarded the *Queen Elizabeth* for the trans-Atlantic crossing to Southampton, England. It is ironic to reflect that, thirty-five years after deserting the British stage to go and seek a new life in America, Stan Laurel was returning in the hope of mending the pieces of his broken fortunes. The worm had turned.

Stan explaining to Ollie how he put his clothes in the washing machine,
and hasn't seen them since. The ones in the tumble-dryer have also disappeared..
(*Queen Elizabeth* — 5th February 1947)

Laurel was accompanied by his fourth wife, Ida (pronounced "Eeda") Kitaeva Raphael – his second *Russian* wife. The two had married as recently as 30th April 1946. Meanwhile, Hardy's third wife, Lucille, was unable to join them, due to hospitalisation for a minor operation, but would be travelling across at a later date. Babe had met Lucille on the set of the 1939 Laurel & Hardy film *The Flying Deuces*, where she was the script and continuity girl.

The reception Laurel and Hardy were to receive – at each and every British town, city, and theatre they stayed or played – was to totally exceed anything they could have hoped for, and even take the management, agents, and bookers by surprise. The reason may be that, in a sense, the war years preserved Laurel and Hardy. The British had been more concerned about their battles with the Germans, than about Laurel and Hardy's battles with Fox and MGM, and were unaware of the comedians' decline. After the declaration of peace, it was as if a pause button had been released; and to find that, out of the recent darkness, this glowing light was about to appear in their midst was more than the fans' excitement could contain. Just the thought of the two funny men instantaneously reminded everyone of happy times, and so to actually see them, in person, would fulfil the vision. Thus, on 10th February 1947, as the *Queen Elizabeth* sailed in to Southampton Docks, Laurel and Hardy were absolutely stunned to see thousands of fans waving and cheering, and whistling their signature tune – *The Cuckoo Song*. The scene was almost identical to their arrival at Southampton in 1932 — but *then* they had been almost at the very top of their profession, whereas *now* they were almost at the very bottom.

But the crowd scenes did not end there. There were to be similar ones every time the comedy couple turned up at a railway station, a hotel, a theatre, or any public event. In some cities – like Glasgow, Edinburgh, and Liverpool – the crowds were so vast and so pushy that they were in danger of causing injury not only to Stan and Babe, but to themselves; and so police on horseback were brought in to control them — tactics normally reserved for rioters!

The crowds at Waterloo (that's the station – not the battle) were so great, and so pushy,
that Hardy got split up from his travelling companions, and sought refuge on this bus.
When the Laurels eventually found him, Ida found it all very amusing.
(Waterloo Station, London – 10th February 1947)

The show debuted in Newcastle, in the North East of England, before coming down to the Midlands a week later to play Birmingham. On the show, Laurel and Hardy were the penultimate act on the bill, with the best of British variety acts completing the rest of the programme. While the other acts performed singing, dancing, impressions, musicianship, ventriloquism, juggling, or acrobatics – Laurel and Hardy reprised *The Driver's Licence* sketch. The full script for *The Driver's Licence* is printed in its American format, in the book *The Comedy World of STAN LAUREL*, by John McCabe. In its British format it was presented in three parts – the twelve minute sketch being added to by a further eight minutes of business, front of tabs, split either side of the sketch. This is how it ran:

Starting off the stage act, front of tabs.

The Boys make their entrance to the accompaniment of *The Cuckoo Song*. Whilst Ollie is addressing the audience, Stan continually interrupts him – the pay-off being that Ollie is standing on his foot.

[AJM: This same routine had been in constant use by Laurel and Hardy almost since their partnership began, and was trotted out at most public events, including their appearances in Britain in 1932, and the ones yet to come.]

A link is then inserted whereby they have to go and renew Ollie's driving licence. As they walk off-stage, the curtains open to reveal the interior of a police station, with an officer sat at his desk. The Boys re-enter, and Hardy informs the officer that he wishes to renew his licence. Asked to fill in a form, Hardy points out that he is unable to write as his arm is in a sling. Laurel can't help, explaining that he "can write, but can't read."

The policeman volunteers to fill in the form, but is sorely frustrated – firstly by Stan and Ollie's answers to his questions, and then by the discovery that Hardy's existing licence was left to him by his grandfather.

The cop next gives them an initiative test, in the form of a hypothetical set of driving conditions. The misguided way the Boys react to his questioning leads to his chasing them out of the police station, and firing a shotgun at their retreating figures. A stagehand then runs on, with the seat of his pants on fire, and there is a blackout.

The cop (played by Harry Moreny) returning Hardy's driving licence – the one left to him by his grandfather.

While the cop is busy giving them a theoretical driving test, Laurel helps himself to the cop's water AND lunch.

After discarding their hats, then putting them on again, Hardy and the cop inadvertently end up wearing each other's hat.

["The hat swap" is a routine Laurel and Hardy had done to good effect in a few of their films, and which they often performed when attending public events.]

The Boys re-emerge front of tabs. Hardy addresses the audience with the words: "We hoped you enjoyed our bit of nonsense," and then croons *Shine on Harvest Moon*, to which Laurel does a soft-shoe-shuffle [a routine taken from the 1939 Laurel & Hardy film *The Flying Deuces*].

Stan follows with the song *I'm a Lonely Petunia in an Onion Patch*, to which Hardy does an eccentric little dance. The Boys then close by wishing everyone 'God Bless,' and Hardy introduces the last act on the bill.

Now that the sketch was well-rehearsed and polished, the Boys were sufficiently confident to play at the world's most-famous variety theatre, the London Palladium. The engagement was for two weeks. Let us hope the sketch wasn't *too weak*!

*The Performer* said of the opening night at the London Palladium (10th March):

It is rarely that Variety top-liners get so uproarious a reception on their first appearance at any particular theatre as that accorded the film couple, Stan Laurel & Oliver Hardy at this house, and it was some time before the pair could even begin to get under way.

The pair have material of no particular strength. Indeed, the script can have caused no wet towels and sleepless nights – but what they do have is the benefit of considerable film following, and in this they score heavily by exploiting to the full the various comedy mannerisms that have endeared them to so many. At the finale of this episode, the duo sang a little, Laurel danced a little, and both seemed not a little overwhelmed at the warmth of their reception.

The *Weekly Sporting Review* revealed some hitherto unknown business which the Boys performed, in which they have a little dig at some of their Hollywood contemporaries:

Coming on to a tremendous ovation, those loveable screen comedians Stan Laurel and Oliver Hardy soon proved their worth as mirth-makers, in that they were as good and as funny as you expected them to be.

Dressed identically as you've seen them on the screen, looking and fooling about exactly as they've been doing for years in their popular pictures, Stan and "Ollie" first go through a kind of cross-talk routine, follow with a typical burlesque – "Applying for a Driving Licence," in which they are splendidly assisted by Harry Moreny – and wind up with a series of skits during which Laurel debunks Crosby and Sinatra, and Hardy does likewise to Astaire!

It's altogether a glorious chunk of tomfoolery and the comedians fully justify all the fuss made over them. If you're lucky enough to get into the Palladium, you'll love every moment "Stan and Ollie" are on the stage.

The business referred to above, wherein Messrs. Laurel & Hardy have a little dig at Messrs. Crosby, Sinatra, and Astaire, does not appear in any extant scripted version, which seems to demonstrate that the new material had been inserted, then tried and tested during the two weeks spent in Newcastle and Birmingham. Unless, that is, it is just an over-egged description of the respective performances of *Shine on Harvest Moon*, and *I'm a Lonely Petunia in an Onion Patch*.

With reviews like these, and others equally praising, Laurel and Hardy were kept on at the Palladium for a third week – and still every seat was filled at the fourteen shows per week. Astonishingly, the Laurel & Hardy Show was next booked into another London theatre, the Coliseum, which is even bigger than the Palladium. If filling that weren't a big enough task, consider that Laurel and Hardy's run there was for FOUR weeks, with

two shows per night plus Wednesday and Saturday matinees. [AJM: Why is an afternoon show called a "matinee" when the word comes from the French for "morning."?]

One would have thought that, by now, every London theatregoer who wanted to see Laurel & Hardy *had seen* Laurel & Hardy – but no! The Hollywood screen comedians next played a week at two other London theatres – the Lewisham Hippodrome, and the Wimbledon Theatre.

By now, however, word of the comedy legends' phenomenal success had spread throughout the rest of England, and Scotland, where theatre managers were clamouring to book this magnificent draw. As a result, further engagements were added, as follows:

Between 12th May and 20th September, Laurel and Hardy played the No.1 circuit of variety theatres; which consisted of the Moss Empire theatres in Glasgow, Edinburgh, Liverpool, and Swindon; the Hippodrome theatres in Dudley, Bristol, and Coventry; along with provincial theatres in Manchester, and Hull; plus theatres in the seaside resorts of Morecambe, Blackpool, Skegness (Butlins Holiday Camp), Southsea, Margate, and Boscombe.

In Glasgow, both comedians acknowledged their Scottish roots by dressing in traditional costume.
(Glasgow Empire – 17th June 1947)

[For a complete account of the 1947 tour, see my book *LAUREL & HARDY – The British Tours*].

Bookings eventually ended back in London, on Saturday 27th September, after a week of concurrent appearances at the Finsbury Park Empire, and the Chiswick Empire.

Originally planned to be just twelve weeks, the 1947 British tour had, by public demand, been extended to thirty-one weeks. During that time, word of Laurel and Hardy's popularity and box-office appeal had spread (or should that be "had *been* spread") to Europe – and so, on 1st October the two former screen comedians crossed the North Sea to play the first of several cities on a European tour – a tour they could never had predicted making when first leaving home.

Hold on to your hats, Boys – this is going to be a bumpy ride.

## CHAPTER 2
### A EUROPEAN DRIVING LICENCE

The North Sea, being virtually enclosed on three sides, may lull one into believing it is a calm stretch of water; but sailors beware, when the elements combine it can kick up a swell huge enough to turn even the most hardy of sea travellers into green-faced quivering wrecks. Thus it was that, nineteen hours after leaving the Essex port of Harwich, the Laurels and the Hardys, plus their small entourage, arrived at the Danish port of Esbjerg with a bad case of *mal-de-mer*. But there would be no opportunity to retire to a hotel where they could lie down and wait for the floor to stop moving; as on the pier, waiting to greet them, was a crowd of maybe up to one thousand fans.

At least a third of the crowd consisted of schoolchildren who, seeing as it was now 9:30am, ought to have been in school. But, because the ferry was three hours late, the children had been waiting since very early morning, and so no-one was going to drag them away before they had set eyes on the world-famous funny men. As soon as Laurel and Hardy were sighted on the deck of the steamer *Kronprins Frederik* (*Crown Prince Frederick*) children and adults alike burst into spontaneous cheering.

Police and Customs were out in force but, even so, it was a struggle to keep the onlookers behind the barriers when the two comedy legends came down the gangplank. Putting aside all thoughts of their sea-sickness, Stan and Babe put on a happy face as they made their way through the lines of spectators, and were rewarded with continuous clapping and cheering.

First port of call was the Passport and Customs Office, where formalities were quickly dealt with and the VIPs welcomed onto Danish soil. They then had to run the gauntlet to the railway restaurant, where tables had been set up to accommodate the obligatory press-conference.

Even after patiently answering trite questions about how they had met; what their favourite film was; if they had ever fallen out? etc., the visitors still weren't able to go and rest, as there was yet a six-hour train journey to make. So, with the last question having being asked; the last autograph signed; the last handshake effected; and the last photograph snapped; the touring company were whisked away on the high-speed train, the *Englænderen* (The Englishman).

Even now, removed from the melee, our subjects couldn't rest, as crowds packed the platform at each station, and shouted, whistled and cheered until the two Hollywood stars appeared at the window of their carriage. At Odense Station, the number of curious spectators was so large that one passenger was pushed off the platform onto the railway tracks below, just as the train was pulling away. Luckily he was able to press himself against the side of the platform and thus escape with only minor bruising. Our victim had no doubt laughed many times at the Laurel & Hardy screen characters taking falls, but Laurel and Hardy watching him, in a real-life fall, wasn't so funny.

When the comedy couple finally arrived at Copenhagen Station, it was 3:50pm – three-hours later than had been scheduled, due to the delayed sea crossing. However, the reception committee, fans, and press alike had waited it out – as had the Aage Juhl Thomsen Orchestra, who then welcomed the VIP party with a medley of Laurel & Hardy film music. After handshakes and hand-waves, and the compulsory tie-twiddling and head-scratching, the two comedians climbed into their awaiting transport — an open-backed Landau carriage pulled by two horses. In regal style they were then were paraded through Copenhagen – a short journey, but during which they were kept busy waving to the thousands of people lining the streets (a spectacle caught on film).

Gøg og Gokke kører fra Hovedbanegaarden under Politiets Eskorte og Publikum s hyldest
Laurel and Hardy run from Central Station under police escort and the crowd's adulation.

At their destination, the Palace Hotel, another huge crowd was gathered, attracted by Erik Parker and Niels Foss playing the Laurel & Hardy signature tune. As they had learned to do from many situations like this, Stan and Babe quickly entered the building and ascended to a first-floor balcony, where they could wave to the vast number of fans below without danger of being manhandled, or even crushed.

On the balcony of the Palace Hotel
(Palads Hotel – City Hall Square)

So NOW could they rest? Well – NO! Being three hours late, their rest time had gone, leaving them with barely enough time to walk into their rooms, do the necessaries, and come straight out again to make the 4:45pm Cocktail Reception, at the Ambassadeur restaurant. There, around one hundred famous Copenhagen faces were assembled – gathered from Danish film- and theatre-land.

Among the guests was AV Olsen, from the Nordisk Film Company, who was credited as having come up with the nicknames "Gog og Gokke" – a name which was in common use for the promotion of the Laurel & Hardy films released in Denmark over the years. (The literal translation is "Cuckoo and Robust") [Robust – Hardy. Get it?]

(Poster for the Danish release of "*Sons of the Desert*")

Also present was the Danish comedy double-act Peter Malberg and Ib Schønberg, who one reporter described as being: "… a striking Danish parallel to the U.S. Team" – which is a bit like saying that coal has a striking resemblance to diamond.

L-R: Oliver Hardy, Ib Schønberg, Poul Reichhardt, Peter Malberg, Stan Laurel

Between the demands to make a speech; shake hands with all the stars and dignitaries; snatch a few drinks; have a bite to eat; and clown for the many photographers; Stan and Babe had to find time to sit down with reporters to answer more trite questions. This book would have been twice as long if every Question & Answer session were included; but, if I show you this one, with all the inaccuracies left in, you will realise why I chose to omit most other Q&A write-ups:

"We always laugh at each other, and we think that we are very funny. It's almost impossible to get a good script for a movie. We have recorded 222 movies together. Our films are broadcast in five languages. Ingrid Bergman is currently the biggest name in American films. Jean Hersholt is our best friend.

We knew nothing of Denmark, we understand that Danes are very intelligent people. From here, we journey on to Stockholm, Paris, South America and Australia."

Laurel looking like a man in the electric chair, begging the executioner not to plug it in.

So, having appeased the whole of the assembled guests and pressmen, the newly-arrived guests were rushed over to a local Danish radio station, where they able to inform a much larger number of Copenhagen residents of their presence in the city. [AJM: No confirmation has been found that Laurel and Hardy's interview was ever broadcast, even though there is an extant recording.]

So NOW could Laurel and Hardy be allowed to go to their respective hotel rooms and rest? Well … er … NO! There was barely time to dash to their hotel rooms, change into tuxedos, and dash out again for yet another function. This one was at the behest of the "Board of Ladies" of the "Danish Actors Alliance" who, at 9pm, treated Laurel and Hardy to a dinner at the Wivex Restaurant.

Stan and Babe were able to rejuvenate their tired bodies by the application of several shots of the Danish drink 'schnapps.' Less immune bodies would have been laid out by the effects, but with Stan and Babe's propensity for drink, it had them rounding off the event by frenetically conducting the Teddy Petersen orchestra, while the audience clapped along in rhythm.

The lady on Ida Laurel's right is believed to be their hostess from "The Danish Actors Alliance."

NOW could they go to bed? Sorry! But the answer is still "NO," for there was "The Midnight Show" to attend, at the Palads Teatret (Palace Theatre – a cinema) – not to be confused with the Palace Hotel where they were staying. This event too had been organised by the Actors Alliance, and at which Stan and Babe were about to pay acknowledgement to their Danish peers.

The show started at 11:30pm, with Laurel & Hardy's spot being at the advertised "Midnight." Their entrance on stage was greeted with tumultuous applause, which continued throughout their patter, singing, and dance routine, and even after they had left the stage. Talk about "singing for your supper."

Since departing the English shore, Laurel and Hardy had made a nineteen-hour sea-crossing; given a press-conference; taken a six-hour train journey; partaken in a parade through Copenhagen; made an appearance on the balcony; attended a Cocktail Party; done another press-conference, recorded a radio interview; and attended an early-evening reception; before finishing off with a Midnight Show. That is a grand total of somewhere around thirty-eight hours of almost non-stop activity. This show business lark certainly demands much more than just standing on a stage for twenty minutes each evening.

Now, finally, they *were* able to go to bed. They would need all the rest it afforded them as, even if they managed to recover from the last two days' exertions, there was still another two days of appearances to make – and that was BEFORE their run of stage shows was to begin.

## COPENHAGEN – Day 2 (Danish = København)

Thankfully, Laurel and Hardy's first scheduled event of Thursday 2nd October was at 2pm, by which time one hopes they were somewhat rested. Rather than a public appearance, this was a private audience with the American minister. Being "private," no information or photographs seems to have been released. Their next visit was to Copenhagen Town Hall, where their host was the Mayor – H.P. Sorensen. One surmises it would have been a guided tour of the Town Hall, during which the Mayor would have narrated its history, and pointed out its architecture and art pieces.

Mayor H.P. Sorensen demonstrating how long the stem of his pipe really ought to be,
to prevent the thatch on his chin from catching fire.

The evening found the Boys back in amongst the public, and in a venue they were better suited to, when they attended a show at "Den Little Kabaret" – for which little is known of "The Little Cabaret."

Friday morning was a visit to a venue which was of much more interest than merely historical architecture, namely – a brewery. The premises of the world-famous Carlsberg Company, brewers of fine lager, is located just a few minutes ride from the town centre of Copenhagen. The property covers a vast estate, housing many beautiful buildings, with a rich history dating back to 1847. Many famous people have paid visits to the brewery, including later ones by Winston Churchill and even Queen Elizabeth II, but I have no doubt that the visitors who spread the most enjoyment were Messrs. Stan Laurel and Oliver Hardy.

(By kind permission of Carlsberg)

Upon arrival, their car was surrounded by scores of visitors, most of whom followed the Laurels and the Hardys inside, to the welcoming sounds of *"The Cuckoo Song."*

But then the VIPs were led to the private confines of the Queen's Hall, with its beautiful mahogany doors and panels, Greek statues, and wall friezes depicting ancient Greek battles. Over a light-buffet luncheon, all four of the Hollywood guests did their best not to offend their hosts, by forcing down copious amounts of Carlsberg lager. What a wonderful gesture!

(By kind permission of Carlsberg)

12

After signing the Visitors Book, the two Hollywood stars walked off their luncheon, with a short tour around the grounds, before leaving.

One would imagine the afternoon was spent having a welcome nap, back at the Palace Hotel.

(By kind permission of Carlsberg)

Friday evening found the two film comedians back at the Ambassadeur restaurant, for a "White-tie Gala Evening" – staged as a fundraiser for "Save the Children." They didn't perform, as such, but their presence alone would have attracted "money" people who could then be encourage to give generously. There was a Laurel & Hardy theme, though, in the evening's entertainment. Dance instructor Borge Kisbys had composed a special party dance, which incorporated certain well-known gestures and steps from Laurel & Hardy films. It was performed to a humorous jingle, with lyrics written by Kai Ewans and Ib Schønberg. Borge Kisby was so confident the dance would be a winner, that he had already sold licenses to fifty Dance Schools throughout the country. Let us hope the money he took went into the "Save the Children" fund. Whether or not Laurel and Hardy actually joined in with the dance is not known.

After three days of almost non-stop public appearances, Charity Shows, and events – where all they got for their singing and dancing was supper – it was time to do what Laurel and Hardy had come to Copenhagen to do – MAKE SOME MONEY. On Saturday evening 4th October they played two shows at the K.B. Hallen. (7pm. and 9:15pm.).

K.B. Hallen – full name Kjøbenhavns Boldklub (Copenhagen Ball Club) – was a multi-purpose venue, built to accommodate sports such as badminton, tennis, basketball, volleyball, and handball. Being basically a large floor area with spectator galleries, it could be adapted to a concert hall, with total seating of three thousand. Opened in 1936, some of the earliest music stars to performer there were jazz legends Louis Armstrong, and Duke Ellington. Later appearances by *The Beatles* (1964) and *The Rolling Stones* (1966) led to it becoming a major rock venue.

Here in 1947, though, comedy was an untried medium, and it was going to take a big act, with a whole load of experience of working such a hangar-sized room, to connect with the audience. Fortunately, Laurel and Hardy had played previous shows in similar-sized venues, both indoor and out, during their tour of major US cities in 1940, 41, and 42. [AJM: Refer to my book: *LAUREL and HARDY – The US Tours.*]

Thankfully, all the experience paid off, and a local reviewer was able to report:

> Inden Gøg og Gokke kom, havde Elga Olga Svendsen fået Salen til at vælte med "Den lille lysegrønne ø" Og, Liva Weel med en Række af sine kendteste Viser, Mogens Davidsen læste Fugl holms Digte, og det var næsten Aftenens bedste Nummer, og Hedvig Volmer og Ole Walbom præsenterede sig som Operette par. Det gik net.
>
> Nu er der jo blevet skrevet så meget om Gøg og Gokke, at det til en Afveksling var rart at se dem optræde. Det skete i Aftes i KB-Hallen.
>
> Først Bifald, så Fløjten, så Trampen i Gulvet, så Bifald, så Fløjten – og [så] Bifald.
>
> Og så først begyndte de to amerikanske Komikers. De stod og snakkede lidt, lavede nogle Gags – og man genkendte det hele [...] de [mange] [Film]. Hoved numret var en [Optagelses prøve] til Erhvervelsen af Kørekort og det gik naturligvis i de kendte Baner, ikke så få kan vel huske Gissemand i den Slags. Men bag alle de voldsomme Bevægelser og Falden-på-Halen har Gøg og Gokke en Splint af den store Komik. De er gode Gøglere i den gamle Stil, man fornam ligefrem Duften af Teater i Luften, det var ægte, og det var morsomt. Sluttelig sang Gokke en lille Sang, og Manden har minsandten også Stemme, og derpå dansede begge to. Det var en sjov Aften, og det var vist også Meningen det hele.
>
> (Kobenhaven – 5th October 1947)

Gotcha! Now here it is in English:

> Before Laurel and Hardy came on, Elga Olga Svendsen won over the audience with "The Little Bright Green Island" and Liva Weel with a series of her best-known Songs; Mogens Davidsen read humorous poems, and it was almost the evening's best number; and Hedvig Volmer and Ole Walbom introduced themselves as an Operatic couple. It went nicely.

The Juhl Thomsen Orchestra ought to have been credited; but *more* conspicuous by their absence from the above write-up were Ib Schønberg, and Wandy Tworek. Maybe Schønberg had not lived up to a previous reviewer's comment that he [and his partner Peter Malberg] were "a striking Danish parallel to the U.S. Team."

Of the "U.S. Team" the reviewer offered us:

> So much has been written about Laurel and Hardy, that it was nice to see them actually perform for a change. It happened last night in KB-Hallen. First applause, then whistles, then stamping on the floor, then applause, then whistles – and then applause.
>
> And then the two American comedians began. They stood and talked a bit, made some gags – and you recognize it all from their many films. The main sketch was a test for the acquisition of a driver's licence, and it used of course their famous routines.
>
> But behind all the slapstick and knockabout humour, Laurel and Hardy still have traces of the great comedians. They are good Jesters in the old style, you sensed even the smell of theatre in the air, it was real and it was funny. Finally Hardy sang a little song, and the man actually has a good voice, and then they both danced. It was a fun evening, and that was the intention of it all.

The following day, Sunday 5th October, saw the two evening shows being repeated at the K.B. Hallen, but with an afternoon show being added at 4pm. There was also a surprise for Stan and Babe following one performance, which Stan revealed some years later in a letter to some friends:

```
                    Sept.11th.'59

Dear Rick & Marie:

I have another act which
was recorded on 'Disc
Record', it was made
during our first
performance in Copenhagen,
Denmark. I'll have a copy
made of that for you, its
very interesting as we
knew nothing about this at
the time - did'nt know the
show was being recorded.
```

On stage at the K.B. Hallen (By kind permission of POLFOTO)

Laurel went on to inform Rick and Marie of the fear he and Hardy had had of performing on this European tour:

```
Before we went to Denmark, we feared the language barrier,
afraid they would'nt understand our English dialoge, so we
eliminated as much talk as possible & replaced it with
pantomime, but to our great surprise they understand everything
we said & we had no trouble at all in that respect - this
stadium was used as a Concert Hall, Stars like Grace Moore
would appear for one or two performances at the most - we
played there five nights - we played a big stadium, over 7,000
people were present.
```

Laurel's last statement is rather ambiguous. Just to make it clear: the attendance figure of 7,000 is for all five shows (i.e. 1,200 average, each evening)? To attract so many paying customers to the K.B Hallen had taken Laurel and Hardy a great deal of promotional time and effort, but the box-office receipts would be stupendous. But something was to go wrong – VERY wrong. So much so that Stan and Babe's long-lasting working-partnership, and even friendship, would very soon be brought into question.

CHAPTER 3

## KEEP STATIONERY

Having achieved five extremely well-attended houses at the K.B. Hallen, Laurel and Hardy had been seen by pretty well all the theatregoing members of Copenhagen's populace. It was time to move on to pastures new. The last six days had been pretty gruelling, but there would be no let-up, as Stan and Babe now had twelve continuous days of shows to perform in different Swedish towns and cities. But first, the day of travel.

## Monday 6<sup>th</sup> October – Malmo, Sweden (Malmö, Sverige)

After making the forty-five-minute ferry crossing from Copenhagen to Malmo, the Laurel and Hardy touring party then boarded a train bound for the Swedish capital, Stockholm. Upon arriving early evening at Stockholm Central Station, the two stars of the group were mobbed by shouting screaming clamouring fans, who soon broke through the police cordon. This totally unnerved Hardy, who was quoted by one reporter as revealing: "I was scared we were going to be trampled in there." So with barely enough time to listen to the brass band playing *The Cuckoo Song*, Stan and Babe dashed for the safety of their limousine, and were whisked away – leaving the mob with only a few head-scratching and tie-twiddling gestures to remember them by.

Leaving the Grand Hotel.

In direct contrast to Laurel and Hardy's gruelling Copenhagen schedule, here in Stockholm they had no first-day appearances to make so, for the first time in over a week, they were able to enjoy the comfort, privacy and rest which their hotel rooms afforded them. Consequently, they awoke Tuesday morning bright and refreshed. Even Stanley looked bright! So much so that they decided to do something they very rarely risked – which was to go for a stroll.

It all started off so well. Leaving the Grand Hotel, in the Östermalm district of Stockholm, the celebrity tourists paused to pose against a statue situated outside the Kungliga Dramatiska Teatern (Royal Dramatic Theatre). From there they strolled along the waters-edge down the Strandvägen (Strand Way).

In the words of the song: "Let's all go down the Strand."

Laurel, being a former boat owner, was delighted when, having passed many small sailing boats, they were invited on board the *Bore*, and given a tour by the Captain – F.C. Jöhnk.

Outside the Kungliga Dramatiska Teatern                On board the *Bore*

But then things went wrong, in the usual way in which events went wrong whenever Stan and Ollie appeared together in public. Laurel, for some reason known only to himself, had a real passion for stationery and, in later life, revealed that he would have loved to have run a stationery shop. Spotting one on the journey back to their Stockholm hotel, he couldn't help but go inside for a browse. Bad move! The shop may have been stationery, but the huge crowd outside didn't remain stationary, and began to push their way inside to get closer contact with the comedy stars. With the word being spread like wildfire that Laurel and Hardy were shopping in town, the situation soon got well out of hand – as people began swarming in like piranhas in a feeding frenzy. Soon, the small police escort they had with them was completely overwhelmed, so reinforcements were sent for to prise the comedy twosome out of the shop, and shove them into a taxi to get them safely back to the hotel. So much for a quiet stroll.

With no crush injuries having been sustained, the Boys were able to make their two scheduled performances that same evening. The venue was the Konserthus (Concert Hall) – designed by Swedish neoclassical architect Ivar Tengbom, and completed in 1926.

The imposing facade of the Konserthus, with its ten huge Corinthian columns.

Some say the building's biggest claim to fame is that, every year since its opening, it has hosted the Presentation of the Nobel Prizes, which are awarded each December by the reigning Monarch of Sweden (excepting the "Peace Prize"). I would prefer to say that its biggest claim to fame is having Laurel and Hardy appear there, but then – I'm biased.

Located near Hötorget, a market square in the heart of Stockholm, "The Concert Hall" is actually comprised of three halls – the Grünewald Hall, named after its designer, Isaac Grünewald, with its magnificent Renaissance interior; the Aulin Hall, named after the Swedish composer Tor Aulin, and finally the largest and less ornate hall, The Main Hall, which was the one chosen to host the Laurel & Hardy Show. The Aulin's 1,770 seating-capacity may seem huge to most acts, but not to Laurel and Hardy. To cater for ticket demand there were going to be ten shows on six out of the next eight evenings — Tuesday 7th to Tuesday 14th October. [That's two shows per night on four evenings, and just one show on each of the last two.] Shows were at 7pm and 9:15pm.

As Laurel and Hardy's total stage time was only around thirty-minutes, support acts were needed to fill the rest of the show's running time. These were Swedish artistes Åke Söderblom and Egon Larrson (themselves a comedy double-act); and Swedish singer Maj-Lis Lüning; with musical backing, and musical interludes provided by the Arne Hülphers Okestre.

Åke Söderblom and
Egon Larrson getting familiar
with the two Hollywood giants.

(A little too familiar, perhaps?)

The review of the Opening Night show ran as follows:

### Helan och Halvan gjorde succé

*Stockholmarna kunde motstå de två populara filimdolerna Helan och Halvan. De lockade fullt hus två gånger å rad i Konserthusets stora sal på tisdagen, och sällan har det väl skrattats så gott i denna sal förut. Det tog visserligen en het timme innan hrr Hardy och Laurel gjorde sin med spänning motsedda entre, men den underhällning som bjöds före var heller inte träkig. Ake Soderblom och Egon Larsson kan också konsten att roa publiken. Förprogram met forgylldes vidare upp av paranta Maj-Lis Luning samt av Arne Hulphers och hans jazzband.*

*Hälsade av en applådstorm som fullständigt dränkte deras kända Coo Coo sång tågade så Hardy och Laurel in, skrudade precis som man ser dem på vita duken. Större delen av spektaklet upptogs sedan av en sketch, där de sökte dupera vederbörande tjänsteman att bevilja dem licens att köra bil. Och det blev ett enda raljant clownen i deras kända stil. Så briljerade Hardy som kuplett sångare och stepp dansor, och slutnumret blev inte minst effektfullt om också litet ovanligt för ess.*

*Den ymniga blomsterskörd som överracktes till dem strödde de nämligen med givmilda händer ut över parketten.*

## Whole and Half were a success

Stockholm residents could not resist the two popular film idols Laurel and Hardy. They attracted a full house twice in succession in the Concert Hall's Great Hall on Tuesday, and rarely has so much laughter been heard in this room before. It was a whole hour before Messrs. Hardy and Laurel made their long awaited excitement-filled entrance, but what was offered before they came on was not boring. Ake Soderblom and Egon Larsson also [art??] to entertain the audience. The pre-programme is made up by the stylish Maj-Lis Luning and Arne Hülphers and his jazz band.

Stan and Babe pointing out the pretty face of singer Maj-Lis Lüning.

Greeted by a huge round of applause, which completely drowned their well-known *Coo Coo Song*, in marched Hardy and Laurel, attired exactly as you see them on the silver screen. Most of the spectacle was then taken up by a skit in which they sought to dupe the appropriate official to grant them a licence to drive a car. And it became one bantering clown in their known style. So excelled Hardy couplet singer and tap dancer, and the final number was not the least effective if a little unusual for the stars.

They were presented with huge bouquets of flowers, which they then scattered among the people in the stalls.

(*Dag Bladet* – 8th October 1947)

The following night, Wednesday 8th October, was one of the two on which Laurel and Hardy weren't performing at the Konserthus. They were, however, still making an appearance. A "Gala Banquet" had been arranged at the Ambassadeur, at which they were to be the Guests of Honour. The event, titled "Filmbal," was hosted by a film publicists company, at which some available Swedish film and show business stars were in attendance. These included: Greta Jacobsson, Lizzy Olosson, St. Erson, Namen Carl-Gustaf Lindstedt, Nils Olsson and Gunnar Lindqvist, George Adelly (Ping Branch), Kai Gullinar (Ping Power) and Gösta Bernhard, Kaj Gullmar, plus Åke Söderblom and Egon Larsson. Many of the known acts did a little party-piece – some of which had been rehearsed; others ad-libbed – while the main floor-show was Gosta Bernhard with the full company from "Casinorevyns" (Casino Revue); all followed by dancing till late.

TOP LEFT:
While Laurel is giving a "Thank You" speech to their hosts, Hardy is praying he won't try to say it in Swedish.

TOP RIGHT:
Surrounding Laurel and Hardy are members of the Casinorevyn, with Kai Gullmar, Gosta Bernhard, Irene Soderblom, and the 3 Knas!

BOTTOM LEFT:
Stan and Babe are amused by something Stig Olins said, while Klasse Thorngrens appears not to get the joke.

BOTTOM RIGHT:
Hardy drinking a toast with m/c Lauritz Falk, while Norwegian Liv Bredal smiles through the cigarette smoke.

There is no doubt that Stan and Babe would have enjoyed the event. Put them where there was food and drink and some lively music, and they were as happy as a pig and a hippopotamus in mud. In this instance it was noted that Laurel, in particular, had a liking for drinking the notably strong Swedish schnapps "brennvin" (which translates as "fire wine"). During his early morning stroll the previous day, Laurel had confessed that he had had no less than seven shots of brennvin; which, though this number may seem excessive, was not as strong as the Danish schnapps he and Hardy had also thoroughly "sampled."

On the third night of the Stockholm engagement, it was back to the Konserthus for two more shows. The fourth night, Friday, was another break in the run at the Konserthus but, again, Stan and Babe filled in the evening at an event. This one was at The Cirkus, located on Djurgårdsslätten. Erected in 1892, The Cirkus was purpose-built in the style of a circus tent; except in brick (hence why it is still a fully-working theatre these one-hundred and twenty-plus years later). Over its life, The Cirkus has hosted plays, musicals, TV productions, conferences, and many rock and pop concerts. Being able

Interior shot of the Stockholm Cirkus.

to easily seat 1,800 people, it rivals the Main Hall in the Konsertus and, with its seating in-the-round, and excellent acoustics, is also an ideal venue for staging intimate shows and plays. Makes you wonder why Laurel and Hardy weren't placed in there.

On this night though, the two great film clowns were there merely as spectators of the premiere of the show *Vi Som Vill Opp*, which translates as something like *We Like to Go Wild* (I think). Upon arriving, and taking their seats, two rows back from the ring, Stan and Babe happened to wave to the compere, Einar Fröding, who immediately climbed down and reached over to shake their hands. Upon returning to the stage, his attempts to welcome the two Hollywood legends – using his own language of Värmland, plus broken English – caused much hilarity.

Compere Einar Fröding welcoming Stan and Babe to the Stockholm Cirkus.

Then it was on with the premiere of the show, which was reviewed as follows:

*Gamla cirkus har skådat mången föreställning med världsartisterna men sällan något så trevligt som "Vi som vill opp". Glatt humör och spelglädje kännetecknade föreställningen från början till slut. Vi kan inte nämna alla men måste absolut ge en eloge åt de yngsta, Monica Melin och Pe-Fe Ericson, otroligt charmiga ungar, som fullständigt erövrade publikens hjärtan, hon med en sång om gojan och kanariefågeln och han med "Mitt svärmeril." En lekfull gosse vid namn Jan Lindblad visade sig vara jonglör av stora mått. Fortsätter han på den vägen är han snart uppe i världs klass. Britt Sofie Hemström gjorde lycka som "Den verkliga divan" och den mystiske herr Kilroy, Ragnar Jahn, inhöstade också applåder.*

*En nästan fulltalig publik med Helan och Halvan i spetsen visade sin livliga uppskattning. Revyn är värd all framgång.*

Titten (*Dag Bladet* – 11th October 1947)

-----0-----

The Old Circus building has seen many a show with international artists, but rarely any as nice as "We Like to Go Wild." Cheerfulness and joy characterized the show from beginning to end. We cannot mention everyone, but absolutely must give credit to the youngest, Monica Melin and Pe-Fe Ericson, incredibly charming kids who completely conquered the hearts of the audience; she with a song about "Polly and the Canary," and he with "My Crush." A playful boy named Jan Lindblad [assisted by Vera Kinigren] proved to be juggler of great talent. If he continues on this path, he will soon be world-class. Britt Sofie Hemström brought happiness with "The Real Diva," and the mysterious Mr. Kilroy, Ragnar Jahn, also reaped applause.

A nearly full attendance audience, with Laurel and Hardy as chief guests, showed their lively appreciation. The Revue is worth every success.

[AJM: Here are a few more of the acts: T.N. Lillia; T. V. Varmtannigen; the aforementioned Einar Fröding; the sailor-wise singing Admiral, Roll Aberg; and the biggest attraction, apparently, Mrs. Hilda Capercaillie, from Pajala, making her debut at the circus theatre!]

Throughout the show, Stan and Babe were noted to be "heartily amused," and to be applauding just as enthusiastically as the rest of the audience. Later on, in the bar-room, they posed for photographs with the acts from the show, and thanked them all for a thoroughly enjoyable evening. I wouldn't have thought the artistes needing much thanking. To be performing in front of two living legends was more than a big enough reward of its own.

Laurel confusing Hardy with "the finger-wiggle."

Saturday found the Boys back at the Konserthus, with shows at 7pm and 9:15pm, while the two Sunday shows were at 2pm and 4:15pm. Stan and Babe would have particularly enjoyed the Sunday afternoon shows, as there would have been a larger representation of children, and it was hearing the children's laughter which brought them additional joy. The run finished with just one show each night at 8pm on the Monday and Tuesday. And that was that – ten shows with seventeen-hundred paying customers at each show. This would have put a few Kronas in the pockets of the overseas visitors – but would they be allowed to keep it?

# CHAPTER 4

SWEDEN SOUR

Next stopover on the Swedish tour was a very strange choice of venue, as it was built for the purpose of EDUCATION – not ENTERTAINMENT. Possibly working on the principle: "All work and no play makes Jack a dull boy" Uppsala University [located fifteen miles north of Stockholm] had recently decided to inject a bit of stage culture into its curriculum, by booking artistes to play in its assembly room – the Aula (hall). The first of these was violin virtuoso Yehudi Menuhin, who performed a concert there on 7th October; so Laurel and Hardy were to be the second lab-rats in this experiment, playing just one night there on Wednesday 15th October.

| Original newspaper clipping | Facsimile in Swedish | English translation |

One newspaper preview ran:

*Helan och Halvan i Uppsala Universitets aula – det låter väl ganska roligt. På onsdag träder hrr Hardy och Laurel in på de bräder som utgör den vetenskapliga världens främsta plattform i Uppsala, där som bekant numera allvarligt syftande teater är portförbjuden. Akademistaten, dvs. professorer och docenter och några få dessutom, har gamla rättigheter att käpa biljett tidigare, och deras köpstart på lördagen visade att Helan och Halvan kan räkna pa en mycket lärd publik på aulans 2,000 platser.*

-----o-----

Laurel and Hardy in Uppsala University Hall - sounds like pretty good fun. On Wednesday Messrs. Hardy and Laurel will be treading the boards that make up the scientific world's premier stage in Uppsala, where, as we know now, serious shows are barred. The Academy of the State, ie. the professors, associate professors [Deans], and a few others, have ancient rights to purchase tickets in advance, and tickets sales since Saturday show that Laurel and Hardy can count on a very scholarly audience filling the Aulan's 2,000 seats.

Sad to say, the prediction that Laurel and Hardy could count on all two-thousand seats being filled, did not come true. In fact, if the attendance figures for BOTH shows were combined, they may well have failed to total two thousand.

One review gave the opinion that:

Helan och Halvan – Slog ej an i Uppsala.

*UPPSALA, onsdag. (Sv. D:s Uppsala-korr.) Helan och Halvans gästspel i universitetsaulan var a priori ett pikanteri, då lokalen brukar vara obevekligen stängd för den allvarligare fru Thalia. De amerikanska filmkomikernas framträdande i kväll förlöpte emellertid programenligt och ingen av Uppsalas många akademiska lärofäder hade ansett mödan värt att bege sig dir. Även studenterna ställde sig kallsinniga till de forna bio-idolerna – tiden rinner fort och det följer ideligen nya smakriktningar.*

*Det var långt ifrån utsålt men den övervägande borgerliga och medelålders publik som mött upp hyllade troget de gamla pajkastarna som tydligen framkallade många goda minnen från slapsticktiden. Däremot verkade den inramning som de amerikanska gästerna bestätts på svenska alltför billig.*

*Åke Söderblom och Egon Larsson kom med mycken gammal skåpmat, som serverades så på bredd att den goda smaken fick sitta åtskillig i klämma. Det går dock inte att leka enkel folkparkskabaret på aulans podium, något som också den arrangerande nöjesbyrån bort betänka. I en annan och mindre pretentiös omgivning hade Helan och Halvan säkert gjort en större succé.*

(*Dag Bladet* – 16th October 1947)

The above review proved very difficult to translate into English. It is actually an old form of Swedish, which no-one under the age of thirty will have been taught. It's the equivalent of a British person of the older generation being brought up on 'old' money, and the younger generation knowing only decimal currency. Here is the best attempt at a translation, after four people had put their brains together:

Laurel and Hardy – Don't go well in Uppsala.

UPPSALA, Wednesday. (A. D's Uppsala corr.) Laurel and Hardy's guest appearance in the university auditorium was prima facie a piquancy, when the premises are usually inexorably closed to the serious wife Thalia. The American film comedians' appearance was considered not worthwhile going to by any of Uppsala's many academic curriculum fathers. The students stood indifferent to the former screen idols – time passes quickly and it continually follows new tastes.

It was far from sold out, but the majority of the bourgeois and middle-aged crowd that turned up faithfully celebrated the old pie throwers, who apparently provoked lots of good memories of slapstick times. However, it seems the Swedish support acts to the American guests were too cheap.

Ake Soderblom and Egon Larsson's material was far too dated, and was wide of the mark of good taste. It is not possible to play public park cabaret on aulan's stage, which is why the organizing entertainment agency removed it from the programme. In different and less pretentious surroundings Laurel and Hardy would certainly have been a bigger success.

Basically, Laurel and Hardy's act had fallen between two stools – the first on which sat the older generation who thought slapstick and "custard-pie throwers" (their words, not mine), was beneath them; and the younger generation who had not been brought up with silent films and/or slapstick. Those between the older and younger generations, aptly name the "middle-aged," seemed to have appreciated Laurel and Hardy's act for its worth. In summary: it was simply the wrong crowd. Ironically, the reasons behind their non-acceptance was the very premise behind the Laurel & Hardy film *A Chump at Oxford* – in which two adult males had been considered as low-class all their lives, simply because they were poorly educated. The current event was almost a case of "life imitating art." But life moves on, and so did the two old stars. They had proved in Stockholm that their talents were still appreciated, and would do so many more times, in different venues, and other countries, soon to come.

-----0-----

## Thursday 16<sup>th</sup> October — Gothenburg (Swedish = Göteborg).

First thing Thursday morning, "Fatty and Lord Paddington" vacated their university dorms, and took a train to Gothenburg. Arriving around midday, they were given a rousing welcome at the station by a crowd of a few hundred, mostly schoolboys clutching autograph books in the hope of getting the two film legends to sign them. But Laurel and Hardy were in no mood to hang around, and, along with their wives and manager, took a taxi to the Palace Hotel, leaving the kids waving their autograph books in vain. Boo!

In the afternoon the city's VIP visitors were interviewed by well-known Swedish radio presenter Sven Jerring for his 'live on air' radio programme *Barnens Brevlådas* (Children's Letterbox). It would appear that what Laurel and Hardy said during the broadcast wasn't of much interest as, in the newspaper review the following day, the only mention was of Sven saying he had been "nicely received" by the two stars, but who then went on to rave about the musical talents of a couple of kids who were on his show. Like the saying goes: "Never work with children …"

In Stockholm, Stan and Babe had been to a show in a circus-style building – a venue which I suggested may well have suited them as performers. Well, here in Gothenburg, they had a chance to test out that theory as they were about to work the Lorensburg Circus — two shows per night (7pm and 9:15pm) for the next two nights.

[AJM. The venue had been purpose built for circus acts but, like its Stockholm counterpart, later became a Rock venue for music artistes such as The Beatles, The Who, and Jimi Hendrix. Sad to report that the Lorensburg Circus was demolished in 1969, and the vacant site used as a car park. Progress, hey!!]

So did the venue suit Laurel and Hardy? This newspaper review should answer that, although the translation may raise other questions.

### Hollywoodgästerna på Cirkus

*Det var en hel del folk, som hade begett sig till Cirkus i går för att möta Oliver Hardy och Stan Laurel i levande livet. Och långt fram i programmet infunno de sig också, den koleriske tjocke komikern och den lille flegmatisk herrn, som alltid visar tillvaron en så befogad misstro. Man har sett Helan skratta sitt stora, diaboliska skratt och sett honom stelna i förargelse över kumpanen, och man har sett borsten resa sig av förskräckelse och häpnad på Halvans huvud i många filmer – och visst har man skrattat åt deras slapsticks i åtskilliga fall och i andra funnit dem generade enkla och upprepade.*

*Det föreföll, som om deras beundrare voro mycket belåtna med dem i går kväll också – även om de rimligtvis måste ha sett, att deras sketch på körkortskontoret var ännu enklare och levde på ännu svagare gags än deras filmscener. Den sketchen motiverade i varje fall ingen resa över Atlanten och har nog ett rätt diskutabelt reklamvärde. Överhuvud är kanske ett sådant utnyttjande, som vi bevittnade i går, av film dukens magiska makt över själarna ett rätt olustigt tidens tecken. Kring jublade blevo emellertid de två skämtarna av en publik, som var ordentligt uppvärmd av ett mycket gott förprogram. Detta låg långt över vad Helan och Halvan hade för sig – utom i den mekaniska rutinen.*

-----0-----

### Hollywood Guests at the Circus

There were a lot of people who went to the circus yesterday to meet Oliver Hardy and Stan Laurel in real life. And far into the program they also found, the choleric [quick-tempered] stout comedian and the little phlegmatic gentleman who always shows life as a justified distrust. They saw Helan [Hardy] laughing his big, diabolical laughter and saw him stiffen in anger over his companion, and you have seen the bristles rise of terror and amazement at Halvan's [Laurel's] head in many movies – and certainly have laughed at their slapstick in several cases and in others found them embarrassed simple and repetitive.

It seemed as if their fans were very pleased with them last night too – even if they reasonably should have seen that their skit on the driver's licence office was even easier and lived on even weaker gags than their movies. The sketch justified in any case no trip across the Atlantic and has probably a right questionable advertising value. It was a sad and unsettling sign of the times to witness yesterday's attempt to exploit the magic of the movie screen. The crowd, however, happily cheered the two comedians, but perhaps that was due to the warm-up act. That part of the show was far better than whatever it was Laurel and Hardy did - with the exception of the well-rehearsed comic routine of the two celebrities.

Hardy taking a sneaky look at the audience, from backstage at the Lorensburg Circus
[Photo by the famous Swedish photographer Lennart Håwi (1920-2003)]

The "very good pre-programme" mentioned in the above review was the same company of support acts as in the previous shows in Sweden; namely Ake Soderblom, Egon Larsson, Maj-Lis Luning, and the Arne Hülphers orchestra. For Laurel and Hardy, though, the shows in Gothenburg were very disappointing on two levels: Firstly, there had been insufficient publicity to inform locals that the Boys were in town, and so they played to half-empty houses. Secondly, it would appear that Laurel and Hardy's Anglo-American humour did not translate too well to the Swedish audiences, and therefore did not provoke the usual laughs.

Stan and Babe must have been seriously questioning what the heck they were doing playing in foreign countries, to audiences whose first language was not English. And in the wider picture came the bigger question: "How come that the USA, with its fifty states of grey – each one bigger than any of the European countries they were visiting – could not supply work to these two legends of the comedy screen?" It remains one of the biggest cases of maltreatment in show business history.

To lift their obvious depression when whiling away their off-stage time, the Boys took to "appreciating" the Swedish drink "Skånsk Akvavit," a kind of schnapps, 47% alcohol, which they reportedly drank in number!

Local journalists conducting an informal interview in the restaurant at the Palace Hotel, Gothenburg.

The Boys in playful mood, backstage at the Lorensburg Circus.

## Friday 17th October — MALMO (Swedish = Malmö)

Thankfully, Stan and Babe didn't have to drive on the morning after drowning their sorrows the night before in Gothenburg. However, how exactly they did get there is unclear. It is known that the rest of the company from the show travelled by train from Gothenburg, arriving at Malmo at 12:45pm. As these details had been published in the local newspaper *Sydsvenska Dagbladet Snällposten*, some three days before the date of arrival, one would have expected a write-up of the usual mob scenes at the railway station. As none were in evidence, one must surmise Laurel and Hardy sneaked in, unnoticed. My own theory, if that is the case, is that they got off the train one stop before Malmo, at Helsinberg, and then took a taxi to the Kramer Hotel, in Malmo.

Their non-appearance at the railway station may well have caused some disappointment, but there was still some excitement in the air at Laurel and Hardy's presence in the city.

*Stan Laurel, "Halvan", gör sin fundersamma favoritgest.*

*Få filmartister ha en så fast och trogen publik – inte minst i Malmö – som Oliver Hardy och Stan Laurel, Helan och Halvan. När de om lördag framträda i Malmö kan man också vänta sig, att de ges ett extra hjärtligt mottagande. Den våldsamma succén i Köpenhamn och Stockholm talar ju sitt tydliga språk.*

*Särskilt roligt är det, att medlemmarna i SDS:s filmcirkel få tillfälle att personligen bekanta sig med de två världsstjärnorna vid sammanträdet på lördag kl. 23 på biografen Alcazar. Denna första sammankomst har fått formen av ett farsprogram med anledning av Helans och Halvan visit.*

*Själva ha Helan och Halvan samma kväll en egen nattiné på annat håll att tänka på. Den äger rum på Palladium och börjar kl. 23.30. Lyckligt nog har det slumpat sig så att deras framträdande på denna nattiné äger rum så sent att de dessförinnan hinna med att besöka SDS:s filmcirkel på Alcazar.*

*I Palladiumnattinén medverka för övrigt goda bekanta till malmöpubliken: Ake Soderblom och Egon Larsson, Arne Hulphers med orkester samt Maj-Lis Luning.*

-----0-----

Few movie artists have such a solid and loyal audience - not least in Malmo - as Oliver Hardy and Stan Laurel, Laurel and Hardy. When they appear on Saturday in Malmö, one can also expect that they be given an extra warm welcome. The considerable success in Copenhagen and Stockholm speaks for itself.

Especially pleasing is that the members of SDS's film circle have the opportunity to get personally acquainted with the two world stars at their meeting on Saturday, 23pm at the Alcazar cinema. This first meeting has taken the form of a father's program on the occasion of Laurel and Hardy's visit.

Laurel and Hardy have their own matinée elsewhere that evening to consider. It takes place at the Palladium and starts at. 23:30. Luckily, it is random so that their appearance at this matinée is taking place so late that they have enough time to visit the SDS's film circle at the Alcazar beforehand.

The Palladium matinée participants are otherwise good acquaintances of the Malmö crowd: Ake Soderblom and Egon Larsson, Arne Hülphers with orchestra and Maj-Lis Luning.

Note that, in Swedish write-ups, Laurel and Hardy are referred to as "Helan och Halvan," which was the winning entry in a competition run by a magazine called *Filmjournalen* to name the Boys. It translates as, "Whole and Half." Unfortunately, someone failed to spot that, to match up to the characters of "Stan and Ollie" the name should have been "Halvan och Helan" – i.e. "Half and Whole." Consequently, in all the Swedish write-ups, Hardy is named as "The Half," and Laurel as "The Whole." DOH!

The favourable light under which Laurel and Hardy had entered Malmo was soon to change to that of a dark cloud. The first shift in mood towards the two comedians came when it was time for them to make a walk-in appearance at the event being hosted by the SDS's Film Circle. It would seem that Stan and Babe had been given no prior notice of this. Had they been informed in good time, they would no doubt have honoured the booking, which had been made by their Europe agent, Valdemar Sorenson. However, as the SDS wanted them at the Alcazar cinema at 11pm, but they were due to go on stage at the Palladium theatre at 10:30pm, they were forced to decline to make the first appearance.

The cinema management then aired their intent to charge Stan and Babe with a breach of contract over the non-appearance at the film screening. However, after accepting that Laurel and Hardy could not be in two places at the same time, and that, had sufficient notice been given, the two stars would have attempted to honour the appearance (but at a different time), the cinema dropped the claim. That wasn't good enough, however, for one particular local journalist. He took the non-appearance as a snub against the non-paying audience, and, tried to make out a case that Laurel and Hardy were in Malmo purely for mercenary reasons. Erasing all references to their extensive film history, and choosing not to inform us as to the merits of the stage show, he misused all of his column space to smear the good reputation these two gentlemen had worked so hard to acquire over their twenty-one year partnership:

*Efter att med pukor och trumpeter ha gjort entré i Sverige visade sig de två amerikanska filmartisterna Laurel och Hardy, mera kända under pseudonymen Helan och Halvan, vara två enkla divor som t. O. M. ansåg det med sitt rykte förenligt att bryta ett avtal att framträda inför SDS:s filmcirkel i går kväll.*

*Den mycket omtalade turnén blev för Sveriges vidkommande ett strålande konstnärligt fiasko, vilket enligt de svenska turnémedlemmarnas egen utsago i hög grad får skrivas på hrr Laurels och Hardy konto. Genom sin omedgörlighet och sin självöverskattning vållade de sin svenske impressario oöverstigliga svårigheter.*

*I Goteborg lyckades man endast samla ¾ hus och pressen var synnerligen missbelåten. I Götebergs Handelstidning skrev redaktör Helge Hignernan bl. A.: "Är det sant att Helan och Halvan uppbära ett honorar av 6,000 kr. pr kväll så måste i anständighetens namn det svenska crazyparet Söderblom—Egon Larsson ha 12,000." Det tyckte säkerligen också publiken på SDS:s filmcirkel i går, som hade furstligt roligt åt de svenska artisterna och inte saknade de amerikanska "absent friends" ett dugg.*

*Dessutom fick publiken tack vare alskvärt tillmötesgående av Malmö Biografaktiebolag och filmofficinen Eagle-Lion vara med om en oväntad förhandsvisning i Malmö av den omtalade engelska storfilmen "Frieda" med Mai Zetterling I huvudrollen.*

*De två herrarnas – Helan och Halvan – gästspel kommer också i en underlig dager rent valutamässigt seit för den, som känner till exempelvis vilka svårigheter överintendent Wettergren och andra svenska kulturpersonligheter haft och ha för att få resebidrag, när man jämfor deras blygsamma anspråk med dessa amerikanska divors vanvettiga honorar under deras fiaskoturné i Sverige. Man har anledning förmoda, att även danskarna efter detta böra bli åtskilligt betänksamma.*

-----0-----

After a glorious arrival in Sweden that did not pass unnoticed by anyone, the two American film artists Laurel and Hardy, better known under the pseudonym of "Helan och Halvan", proved to be nothing more than two simple divas that even had the impertinence of breaking an agreement to appear before SDS's film circle last night.

The much-hyped tour was to Sweden, a brilliant artistic fiasco which, according to the Swedish tour members' own admission, largely be attributed to Messrs. Laurels and Hardy account. Through their inflexibility and self-overestimation caused their Swedish impresario insurmountable difficulties.

In Goteborg they managed to collect only ¾ houses and the press was extremely dissatisfied. In Gothenburg's Handelstidning wrote editor Helge Hignernan among others. A.: "Is it true that Laurel and Hardy receive a fee of 6,000 kr. pr night so must in the name of decency, the Swedish crazy couple Soderblom-Egon Larsson have 12,000?" We thought surely the audience on SDS's film circle yesterday, who had wined amused by the Swedish artists and not missing the U.S. "absent friends" at all.

In addition, the audience thanks to the kind courtesy of Malmö Cinema Ltd and filmofficinen Eagle-Lion to be part of an unexpected preview in Malmö the famous English blockbuster "Frieda" with Mai Zetterling in the lead role.

The two men - Laurel and Hardy - guest appearances will also be in a strange light purely monetary terms, speaking to those who know the example of the difficulties Superintendent Wettergren and other Swedish cultural figures have had to get a travel grant, when comparing their modest claims with these U.S. divas insane fees for their fiasco of a tour in Sweden. We have reason to believe that even the Danes after this ought to be considerably reluctant.

Methinks the gentleman doth protest too much. He could so easily have written something on the lines of … "It's such a shame that a mix-up by their tour manager resulted in Laurel and Hardy being unable to fulfil the invite given them by the SDS Film Circle, as its members were really looking forward to entertaining these two legends of the silver screen." So to try to totally destroy them as both film stars, and lovely men in real life, was totally uncalled for. That's journalists for you.

[Bibbi Johansson, now a freelance journalist, who spent twenty-one years on the staff of the newspaper company *Aftonbladet*, commented to me:

I have often found in older reviews, that the writer doesn't want to show his readers he is impressed by the big stars who come to Sweden. I once read some reviews of Frank Sinatra, who made a tour around Sweden in 1953. The reviews are so mean, they call Sinatra "a simple crooner with not much of a voice," and they state that "his glory days are over." Well, history proved them wrong.

It cointanly did! – as was the case with Laurel and Hardy, so we won't take it personally, but accept it as the culture of the times.

The Malmo show was the last on the short tour of Sweden, which was perhaps as well, considering that things had turned a little sour. But there was to be worse to come when Stan and Babe tried to leave Sweden and return to Denmark. Upon arrival at the ferry terminal they were stopped and asked to declare how much, in Swedish currency, they were taking out of the country. There was a strict currency allowance in force to prevent Sweden's economy being undermined by unscrupulous traders, bankers, and criminals laundering money illegally gained from countries involved in the recent World War. When the amount of money Laurel and Hardy were wanting to take out was revealed to be well over the maximum amount of Krona allowed, the offence came under the banner of "smuggling."

As our two comedy pals were merely carrying money which the Swedes had more than happily handed over to them, common sense again prevailed, and they were allowed to leave with their egos deflated, but their wallets bulging.

CHAPTER 5

## THE ROYAL COUPLE

From Sweden, the Laurel and Hardy party returned to Copenhagen for an unplanned, and unexpected, reason — an additional three bookings at the K.B. Hallen. These were duly played on Sunday 19<sup>th</sup> October, at 3, 7, and 9:15pm.

Laurel had been thrilled by the attendance at the five shows on their first visit to Copenhagen, so must have been ecstatic to be brought back "By Public Demand." What a contrast to their recent shows in Sweden, which had been poorly attended, and where Stan and Babe's personal ethics had been brought into question.

But then, just as quickly as they had been put back on their pedestal, the two former screen stars were brought crashing down to earth again. The reason why was revealed in this letter, written some twelve years later by Laurel:

Sept.11th.'59

Dear Rick & Marie:

Incidently the producers of the show got into some financial difficulty & to make a long story short, they still owe us $10.000. We heard later that they had gone bankrupt, so thats the end of that. The stadium was packed full every show, too bad we did'nt collect after each performance - unfortunately our manager was'nt with us, as he always handled our business affairs. Anyway, 'Come easy Go easy'.!!

It may seem funny, at first, that Laurel could make light of such a huge financial loss, by dismissing it with a line from their film *Fra Diavolo*, but it was Laurel's totally cavalier attitude, and total lack of business savvy which severely irked Hardy. One must remember that the two of them weren't spending these months away from home to win a popularity contest. Both had huge financial debts which, if not paid, would result in a major downturn in their standard of living, not to mention having severe legal repercussions. So Hardy could rightly feel anger that, after all the hardship endured; all the work put in; and all the money they had earned from the tens of thousands of fans who had paid to see them; it had all been for NOTHING.

Although one could defend Laurel by pointing out that it wasn't his fault the venue company had gone bankrupt, it didn't help that, on a similar tour of England and Scotland in 1932, Hardy had been denied a split of the £30,000 the two of them should have been paid – for which Laurel *was* to blame. But we won't go into that!

There is an unconfirmed report that, the day after the Copenhagen shows (Monday 20<sup>th</sup> October) Laurel and Hardy played a show, or shows, in Hälsingborg (now known as Helsingborg). It is possible that, following a road trip and ferry crossing, the touring show *could* have made it to this small fishing port, but as Hälsingborg is in SWEDEN, it is more likely that the visit there would have been a little earlier – most likely in between the Uppsala, Gothenburg, and Malmo dates. It becomes even more questionable that the Laurel & Hardy Show was hosted in Hälsingborg on Monday 20<sup>th</sup> October as, on the Tuesday, the company was in Aarhus – for which a starting off point from Copenhagen seems far more logical.

### Tuesday 21<sup>st</sup> October — AARHUS (Danish = Århus)

Aarhus is the second-largest city in Denmark and the country's main port. It is located on the east coast of the Jutland peninsula, northwest of Copenhagen, which involves a one hundred and sixteen mile journey by road and ferry to get to. There were two performances per night at the Aarhus Hallen, at 7pm and 9:15pm, on the Tuesday and the Wednesday.

On the day of their arrival in Aarhus, journalist Arnold Bundsgaard, from the newspaper *Aarhus Stiftstidende* interviewed the two comedians, over breakfast, at the Hotel Royal, of which he wrote:

> Breakfast was bacon and eggs. Laurel broke a piece of pastry into pieces and mixed it together with eggs and bacon. He got an angry glance from Oliver Hardy and a comment that they were among decent people and not at home in Hollywood. Laurel was so frightened that he dared not eat, but contented himself with a Pilsner lager.

I shall leave readers to decide if the above counts as professional journalism, or just gross incompetence. We did however learn a little more of the Boys' movements, when we were informed that, later in the day, the comedy couple had a game of bowls in the "Kammeraternes Kegle Club," in Paradisgade. ["Comrades Bowling Club" in Paradise Street]. Using all the journalistic skills I learned from Mr. Arnold Bundsgaard, I offer you my account of how the scene may have played out:

Mr. Laurel bowled a ball, and Mr. Hardy gave him a glance of disdain.

How's that?

Thankfully, we do have an extant photo of the comedy duo, which shows them posing with a group of Aarhus schoolchildren, and for that piece of recorded evidence we must be grateful, and move on — little the wiser.

(Originally published in *Stars and Stripes*.)

## Thursday 23rd October — ODENSE

Next stopover was Odense, Denmark's third-largest city, located on an island sandwiched between the mainland and the one on which Copenhagen stands – which took the Laurel & Hardy Co. a sixty-mile car drive, and a crossing on the night ferry, to get to. That evening they played two shows, at a venue known as Fyns Forsamlinghus (the Village Hall), and two more on the second night. Amazing to think that, in Copenhagen, they could fill a huge stadium many times over, and yet here were consigned to a Village Hall.

Again, we remain frustrated by the lack of newspaper coverage but, thanks to the recently discovered website "www.fynskebilleder.dk," we are at least blessed with pictures of the two stars being entertained by the committee members of another "bowling club" – this one at Naesby, on the outskirts of Odense:

*Fyns Reklame forening havde fået fine gæster ved klubbens kegle spil i Næsvyhoved Skov, og de var gode til at spille kegler. De blev udnævnt til æresmedlem af Fyns Reklame forening og fik et die plom og medalje med deres eget bille de.*

They were appointed honourable members of the bowling club by Fyns Reklameforening (local businesses), and received medals and a diploma with their own pictures on.

Chris James, ace researcher of Laurel and Hardy's appearances in Sweden, was able to expand on what exactly Stan and Babe were presented with. He tells us:

> The visit to the bowling alley, arranged by Fyn's Advertising Association, was on the day of arrival in Odense. There, both comedians received a special two-Krona coin – Ollie's with his face on one side and the King of Sweden's face on the other. Likewise, Stan got one, only with *his* face on one side. (You can see Hardy's pinned on his lapel in the top photo, p115).
>
> That evening, Stan and Babe made a nice gesture at the end of the show, when they sang "Happy Birthday" to the compere, Ib Schonberg.

As for Odense, itself, one website describes it as:

> The quirky, millennium-old capital of Fyn (or Funen), Odense is populated by street corner sculptures of trolls and monster-footed benches. Hans Christian Andersen's birthplace is crammed with fairy-tale-related attractions.

Considering that some of the Laurel & Hardy films were pretty close to the genre of fairy tales – namely *Fra Diavolo*, *The Bohemian Girl* and, of course, *Babes in Toyland* – one might expect the local press to make something of a fuss of the visiting film stars. But that the main story comes from the mention of the game of skittles in the small clubhouse in Naesby, is

Twin bowlers.

the England equivalent of Laurence Olivier playing *Richard III* in Stratford-upon-Avon, and the press writing only that he'd played a game of conkers at the local scout hut in a nearby village.

On Saturday 25th October, the travel-weary comedians again returned to Copenhagen. There were no more shows to fulfil, and thus no need to advertise their presence in Copenhagen, but, even so, one of the first things Stan and Babe did upon arrival was to make a live broadcast on a radio programme called *Weekend-Hytten* (Weekend Hut) – hosted by Svend Pedersen. Hopefully, this "hut" had better content than just a skittle alley!

Laurel and Hardy were to spend the next three days in Copenhagen, but

press coverage had by now deteriorated from "low key" to "lost key," as nowhere could any be found. However, thanks to Peter Mikkelsen we now know that, on one of these nights, Laurel and Hardy attended a gala reception for the "Save the Children" fund. One must presume the reason they did the radio show was to make an appeal on behalf of the fund. At the Gala itself, they were guests of the chairman, who was no less than Prince Viggo – Count of Rosenberg, along with his wife (a commoner) Princess Eleanor Margaret.

A revelation about other occasions when Stan and Babe dined with Royalty came from Laurel himself, in this letter written Sept.11th.'59:

> Dear Rick & Marie:
>
> [The shows at the KB Hallen, Copenhagen were attended by ...] members of the Royal Family who entertained us at their home during our visit a couple of times, Prince & Princess Harold of Denmark & their Son Prince Ulof, he came to the show several times & we became very good friends, it was a wonderful experience meeting all the dignataries of the Country, the party's lasted till the early hours of the AM, we were royally entertained.

[AJM: For fear of being unable to successfully decipher the full lineage of the Danish Royal Family, I shall limit my comments about the Laurel letter to the sketchiest of detail, as follows:

Head of the Royal household was Danish Prince Harald Christian Frederik (born 1876), son of *His Majesty* Frederick VIII – King of Denmark 1906–1912. Harold's wife, Princess Helana, had only very recently been allowed to return to Copenhagen from exile, in order to care for her seventy-one year-old husband who was in poor health. Also in residence were the aforementioned Prince and PrincessViggo, for whom the palace/villa/mansion had been specially built in 1918.

Harold and Helana had five children, two of their sons being Gorm Christian Frederik Hans Harald (born 1919), and Oluf Christian Carl Axel (born 1923). The latter is obviously the one whom Stan refers to as Prince Ulof, who came to watch the show at the K.B. Hallen.]

Back to their last night in Copenhagen (Monday 27th), where Laurel and Hardy were being "royally entertained" by Prince Harold: After dining, evening turned into night, and night turned into early morning, and it was 2:30am before the party broke up. It may well have gone on for longer, had the visitors not had a train to catch, for which Prince Harold and his son Oluf graciously drove them to the station, and waved them off.

When Laurel and Hardy first arrived in Copenhagen they had been treated like royalty. Now that they were leaving, they were being seen off by actual royalty. But then that is quite fitting for "The Kings of Comedy."

# CHAPTER 6

## KING AND COMEDY

On 28<sup>th</sup> October, four and a half hours after leaving Copenhagen, and having crossed over the border into Germany, our nocturnal travellers had to change trains in Hamburg. And that, dear readers, is the answer to the question I have been asked many times over the last two decades: "Did Laurel and Hardy ever visit Germany?" Considering that both Britain AND America had been at war with Germany just two years previously, I doubt that Stan and Babe had it in their hearts, pure and kind as their hearts were, to go and "entertain the troops."

The next change of train would be in Jeumont, France, some eleven and a half hours away – giving the Laurels and the Hardys a chance of getting some sleep. Because of its positioning North of Paris on the France-Belgium border, Jeumont railway station is an important junction for trains travelling into and out of France. To the South is Paris, and to the West is the line to Calais, taken by those bound for the cross-Channel ferry port to England. It also provides connections for Charleroi, Brussels, Ghent, and Antwerp, to the immediate East – all four of which Laurel and Hardy would be visiting after their stay in Paris.

While the two Hollywood comedians were awaiting their connection to Paris, one enterprising cameraman shot some footage of them by the trackside, for which they attempted to improvise some comedy by employing "the hat swap routine" (*ibid*). One humourless member of the crowd, however, felt that Hardy pinching the Jeumont station guard's hat was an affront to dignity and, with malice aforethought, ran in and quickly replaced the hats on the relevant heads. It was one of those moments when one wished that Laurel & Hardy had revived the custard pie tradition of deflating pomposity.

With a damper having been put on the comedy stars' antics it was a relief when the train finally pulled in, thus removing the necessity for further improvisation to appease the crowd's natural expectations.

With the four-hour train journey from Jeumont to add to their travel times, and a three-hour delay to factor in, it was well over twenty fours after leaving Copenhagen before our comedy subjects finally arrived in Paris. All they wanted was get to their hotel, freshen up, and take a well-earned nap on a bed that didn't bounce them around, nor have the accompanying sound of incessant rattling. No chance! A contemporary newspaper article describes the scene upon arrival on the platform of the Gare du Nord Station:

*... un bataillon de reporters attend le rapide de Copenhague qui a plus de trois heures de retard. Et, tout de suite, la bataille s'engage, Georges Jouin, le micro au poing, tente de leur faire dire quelques mots. De toutes parts, on les presse de questions «originales». Les photographes les éclaboussent de magnésium de la tête aux pieds. La foule de curieux qui piétine depuis trois heures les serre de trop prés. Et deux musiciens imberbes jouent «La Marche des Coucous» sur un ton un peu fausset.*

-----0-----

… a battalion of reporters awaits the express from Copenhagen which was more than three hours late. And, immediately, the battle begins. Georges Jouin, with microphone in hand, tries to make them say some words. From all sides, they are pressed to answer "original" questions. There is a constant flash of bulbs from the cameras of the photographers. The packed crowd of curious onlookers have been stamping their feet for three hours. And two beardless musicians play "The March of the Cuckoos" in a high-pitched tone.

Well the Boys certainly look
happy to be in Paris.

The arrival at the Gare du Nord was also filmed, most likely by the same cameraman who had caught our Boys at Jeumont. In the welcoming committee was Pierre Louis-Guérin, the co-producer of the Lido show, who, along with his lovely wife, next escorted them to the theatre.

Gare du Nord, PARIS – 28th October 1947
L-R: Mrs. Louis-Guérin, Ida Laurel, Stan, Babe, Lucille Hardy, and Pierre Louis-Guérin –
who look like they're off to see the wizard, whereas they are actually off to see the Lido.

It would seem that at least one reporter gave up trying to extract an interview from the two Hollywood comedians on the platform, and made the wise move to follow the party to the Lido de Paris, from where he compiled this report:

*J'ai retrouvé les deux compères débarrasses de leur pardessus de voyage et de leurs encombrantes valises au bar du Lido. Ils sont toujours accompagnés de leurs respectables épouses qui ressemblent aux héroïnes des «mariages» de Laurel et Hardy.*

I found the two comedians removed of their overcoats from the journey and their cumbersome bags at the bar of the Lido. They are always accompanied by their respectable wives who resemble heroines of the "marriages" of [the film characters of] Laurel and Hardy.

*Oliver, le premier, répond à mes questions:*

*«Bien sûr, que je suis ravi de retrouver Paris. J'y avais passé seulement deux jours et c'était en 1932. Mais, c'est curieux, les Français ne ressemblent pas à ceux qu'on voit dans les films de chez nous.»*

Oliver is the first to respond to my questions:

"Certainly, I am delighted to be back in Paris. I have spent only two days here, and it was in 1932. But, it is curious, the French do not resemble those which one sees in films back home."

-----0-----

The two days Hardy (and Laurel) had spent in Paris in 1932, came about thus: Between 23rd July and 24th August, Stan and Babe were in Britain. For the first two weeks there was a "Laurel & Hardy Film-Fest" running, in the form of Laurel & Hardy film shorts being played at numerous cinemas throughout England and Scotland. During this two-week period, the two stars made a whistle-stop tour of major cities to help ramp up the film promotion. The third week onwards, however, had been designated as time-out in Paris. Whilst Stan and Babe were being seen off at Victoria Station on 10th August, for the first leg of their journey to Paris, Hardy, assured those present that he was going to rest when they left England, and expounded: "We shall stay in Paris for ten days, and hide from everyone." It was not to be.

Still in 1932, and after disembarking from the *Golden Arrow* train in Paris, the party was ushered into the French Customs Office. This ought to have

The calm before the storm.
(Gare du Nord, PARIS – 10th August 1932)

been a temporary refuge from the assembled mob, but led to the debacle of fans climbing over obstacles and furniture to get near the two stars.

Upon emerging they were picked up by a car, which had been sent by no less a person than the President of France, Albert François Lebrun, and were driven like national heroes down the Champs Elyses – with at least one newsreel camera there, to catch the action. Concurrently, Claridges Hotel gained a great deal of publicity by letting it be known that Laurel and Hardy were staying as their honoured guests, free of charge.

But it was publicity like this that Stan and Babe wished to avoid. Now that everyone knew they were in Paris, and exactly where they were staying, they could find no peace. Reluctantly, after only two days, they gave up, and – also cancelling their planned 1932 sightseeing/promotional tour of Deauville, Berlin, Antwerp, Brussels, and Madrid – returned to London to see out the rest of their holiday time.

[AJM. You can read the full account of Laurel and Hardy's 1932 British tour, along with the post-war tours of variety theatres, in my book: *LAUREL & HARDY – The British Tours*.]

Claridges Hotel – where the manager is about to serve up a storm in a tea cup. (PARIS – 10th August 1932)

Laurel had also visited Paris in 1927 – a little-known trip which came about like this: When the Hal Roach Studios broke for their annual summer holidays in July 1927, Hardy took his wife Myrtle on a long sea voyage from Los Angeles to Havana, Cuba. Laurel, meanwhile, took his new wife Lois on an even longer sea voyage – from New York to Southampton, England. Stan had married Lois a little under a year earlier (23rd August 1926), but his heavy work schedule had allowed no time for a honeymoon. This trip, then, was to serve as both a belated honeymoon, and an opportunity for Stan to be reunited with his father and sister, whom he had not seen since before leaving England in October 1912. Obviously, it would also allow Lois to meet her father-and sister-in-law, plus any other members of her new family the two of them ran into.

The Laurels set sail from New York Harbor on the White Star liner the *Homeric* on 2nd July 1927, and disembarked at Southampton seven days later. After spending a few days with Stan's father, Arthur Jefferson, in Ealing, West London, the honeymoon couple journeyed north to Grantham, Lincolnshire, to see Stan's sister, Beatrice Olga. On 14th July a return to London saw the Laurels making the very surprising move of flying (Yes! "flying") from Croydon Airport to Paris. After enjoying a thirteen-day honeymoon in one of the world's most romantic cities, the satiated couple sailed home on 27th July 1927 from the French port of Cherbourg, aboard the White Star liner *Majestic*.

[Postscript: Because Stan had taken the extended holiday in Paris, he was a week late for the re-commencement of shooting at the Hal Roach Studios. Consequently, he was left out of the film *Love 'Em and Feed 'Em*, and his part given to Max Davidson. One can only imagine how much better the film would have been with Laurel in the role.]

-----0-----

Back to 1947, where the French newspaper article continued with Hardy informing readers:

«*Je ne connais pas Jean Paul Sartre, mais j'aime bien Fernandel. J'ai aussi entendu parler du Tabou. Qu'est-ce que c'est au juste?*»

"I do not know Jean Paul Sartre, but I like Fernandel. I have also heard of Tabou. Is that correct?"

And continued:

*«Je n'ai jamais fait d'émission régulière à la Radio américaine. On nous a seulement interviewé dans les studio de la N.B.C. D'ailleurs, je préfère la télévision et Stanley aussi. N'est-ce pas Stanley?»*

I have never made regular broadcasts on American Radio. We were interviewed only in the NBC studio. Moreover, I prefer television, and Stanley does too. Don't you Stanley?"

*Stan Laurel approuve et enchaine:*

*«Nous effectuons actuellement une tournée à travers l'Europe et nous resterons quelque temps à Paris, où nous jouerons deux fois par jour un sketch en anglais. Oliver chantera et je ferai les claquettes.»*

Stan Laurel agrees and links up:

"We are currently carrying out a tour across Europe and we will remain some time in Paris, where twice per day we will play a sketch in English. Oliver will sing and I will tap-dance."

*«Oui, il a été en effet question que nous tournions un film à Hollywood avec Charles Trenet, mais le scénario ne nous convenait pas. Il ne suffit pas de se jeter á la figure des tartes á la crème pour faire un bon film, n'est-ce pas Oliver?»*

"Yes, sure enough, we have been asked the question if we are going to make a film in Hollywood with Charles Trenet, but the script was not right for us. It is not enough to throw custard pies at someone to make a good film, is it Oliver?"

The press photo identifies this lady as Hardy's wife. He wishes! Although Lucille Hardy was a lovely lady, in every sense of the word, she could never compete with this unnamed young lady, who has beauty and youth comparable with that of Brigitte Bardot in her prime. Methinks she, too, was a French starlet.

A second newspaper article, gained from an interview at the press conference, adds a little more information, but then a little mis-information.

*Après une arrivée sensationnelle hier à la gare du Nord (4 heures de retard – 4,000 personnes attendant) Laurel et Hardy sont allés diner au Lido. Oliver Hardy, le gros et Stan Laurel, le maigre, en béret de parachutiste, ne voulaient absolument pas aller se coucher. Mais leurs femmes respectives les extrayant de l'ascenseur de l'hôtel, les empêchèrent de goûter plus avant aux joies du «Gay Paris» où ils étaient venus une fois seulement passer deux jours en 1932. Laurel et Hardy sont invites à Londres pour assister aux fêtes du mariage de la Princesse Royale et en attendant de repasser la*

*Manche ils comptent visiter Versailles, le Louvre et les grand couturiers. Puis ils reviendront à Paris pour se «produire» pendant un mois devant les Parisiens.*

-----0-----

After a sensational arrival yesterday at the North Station (4 hours delay - 4,000 people were waiting) Laurel and Hardy went to dine at the Lido. Oliver Hardy and Stan Laurel, the thin one, in a parachutist's beret, absolutely did not want to go to lie down. But their respective wives, extracting them from the elevator of the hotel, prevented them from tasting more of the joys of "Gay Paris," where they had come once only to spend two days in 1932. Laurel and Hardy are invited to London to attend the celebrations of the marriage of the Royal Princess and while waiting to cross the English Channel again, they intend to visit Versailles, Louvre and the designer-fashion dress shops. Then they will return to Paris "to appear" for one month in front of the Parisians.

Laurel and Hardy giving a wave of approval to the poster advertising their appearance commencing on 7th November – on stage at 5pm and 9pm.

The statement that Laurel and Hardy had been invited to attend the wedding celebrations of the Royal Princess is slightly inaccurate. The wedding was scheduled for 20th November 1947, at Westminster Abbey, but that is not where the Boys were off to. Their invite was to appear on the annual *Royal Variety Performance* – a fundraising event starring many of the top acts in show business from Britain and overseas, in the presence of members of the British Royal Family.

The Royal Show was to be on Monday 3rd November 1947, at the London Palladium, only four nights before the opening of Laurel and Hardy's own show at the Lido de Paris. Although they had no appearances scheduled before then, the Lido manager used contractual rights to insist that they get to London and back within forty-eight hours. Just to make sure they did return in time – he went with them. So, in the early morning of Sunday 2nd November, Stan, Babe, their wives, and Pierre Louis-Guérin took the boat train to Calais, followed by a ferry across the English Channel, to Dover – on the Kent coast. This was to be a flying visit – but without flying.

[AJM: There is extant footage of Laurel and Hardy and their wives aboard a train, sitting in the dining-car waiting to be served a meal. The voice-over informs us that Laurel and Hardy are on their way to England to appear on the *Royal Variety Show* – but that just isn't so. The footage was actually shot four days earlier, on the train carrying them from Jeumont to Paris. Pathé must have thought that using existing film would be a cheaper option than shooting new footage.]

Doing the *Royal Variety Show* meant a return to the London Palladium, a venue Laurel and Hardy had conquered earlier in the year. This night, though would prove to be a whole new challenge, as it was to be in the presence of King George VI and Queen Elizabeth (the Queen Mother), and their younger daughter – Princess Margaret. The occasion was further marked by the first public appearance, after the announcement of their engagement, of Lieutenant Philip Mountbatten and Princess Elizabeth (now Prince Philip and Queen Elizabeth II).

*The Stage* said of Laurel & Hardy's entrance onto stage:

> Their first appearance in front of the curtain was the signal for a burst of cheering, and the Royal party seemed to know their work and worth.

ROYAL VARIETY SHOW – London Palladium – 3rd November 1947
Laurel and Hardy (seventh and eighth from the right) in the finale line-up, along with:
The Crazy Gang, Gracie Fields, and Tommy Trinder – to name but a few.

Backstage, after Laurel and Hardy had performed their sketch, Charlie Henry (Chief of Production) told them he had observed the King during their act: "… laughing long and loud – throwing his head back while laughing in great appreciation." Stan and Babe would have liked to have been told this first-hand, but were disappointed in missing the opportunity to be presented to the King and other members of the Royal Family, immediately after the show, as they had to dash from the theatre to make the train connection for the ferry back to France.

Another regret has to be that the BBC did not do a radio broadcast of the show. The reason given, by the BBC, was that they were unwilling to pay compensation to other theatres for loss of revenue. Which begs the question: "Why did the BBC not record the show, and broadcast it at a later date, outside theatre hours?"

So, from the *Royal Show* at the London Palladium it was, for Laurel and Hardy, straight into the *Revue Show* at the Lido de Paris. It was going to feel like taking a cold shower after a hot bath.

CHAPTER 7

## REVUE AND REVIEWS

Of Laurel and Hardy's opening show at the Lido de Paris (7th December 1947), one newspaper reviewer wrote:

*Ta, ta, ta, Taratata ... Sur le leitmotiv de l'air qui préfigure et les annonce dans leurs films, l'orchestre prélude a leur entrée. Les voici, pareils à eux-mêmes, tels qu'ils vivent dans les innombrables images que nous gardons d'eux. Stan Laurel sa démarche hésitante, sa malice ahurie, son doux sourire résigne à voiler une feinte innocence; Oliver Hardy, débordant de partout, le nez épaté sur la brosse étroite de la moustache, double ou triple menton, bedaine joyeuse, cravate au vent ... Il suffit de les voir; c'est toute une anthologie filmée du rire qui pénètre avec eux et déchaine la gaiete d'une salle comble.*

*Ont-ils besoind de parler, ces mimes étonnants que seul surclasse le génie humain de Chaplin? Avec le concours de Jacques Henley, à l'intarissable bagout de policier prolixe comme la bêtise de l'Autorité, ils vont déclencher le mécanisme des menues catastrophes dont leur vie est pleine, et la pantomime de leurs gestes des doigts, de leurs regards suffit à provoquer des hilarités sans fin ... Après deux courtes danses cocasses, ils s'en vont, poursuivis par les rappels prolongés.*

-----0-----

The Boys clowning around with the Lido's 16-piece TONY PROTEAU Orchestra.

Ta, ta, ta, Taratata ... The signature tune which precedes their movies, is played by the orchestra as a prelude to their entry. Here they are, like themselves, as they exist in the countless images that we keep of them. Stan Laurel his unsteady gait, his [malice daze], his sweet smile resigned to hide feigned innocence; Oliver Hardy, overflowing everywhere, flat nose on the narrow brush moustache, double or triple chin, potbelly, tie in the wind ... just see; it's a whole anthology of filmed laughter which penetrates with them and unleashes the gaiety of a packed house.

Do they need to speak, these amazing mime artistes that even outperform the human genius of Chaplin? With the help of Jacques Henley, the endless patter wordy police officer as the stupid figure of authority, they will trigger the mechanism of minor disasters that life is full of, and their pantomime of their finger gestures, their glances are sufficient to cause endless hilarity ... After two short funny dances, they leave to prolonged applause.

The rest of the show was also appraised:

*On ne les* [Laurel and Hardy] *reverra qu'au final de Made in Paris, floor-show d'une cadence endiablée dont Daisy Daix est la belle et dynamique vedette et dont châque numéro atteint à une sorte de perfection : exquise distinction de Florence et Frédérique, qui joignent la force de l'acrobatie au style romantique de la danse; comique du duo dansant de Fokkers; surprenant Charlivel don't on ne sait s'ils sont plus cascadeurs que danseurs ou musiciens, alternant des accords de chopin et des triple sauts périlleux, des ensembles de tourbillons et des soli de pirouettes affolantes, grâce exquise des Mears Felton Girls, des modeles et des danseuses tour à tour issus d'une fête galante de Versailles ou du Carnaval brésilien .... Tout un spectacle qui, à une présentation entre toutes raffinée et luxueuse, joint ces qualitiés premières; le rythme de l'ensemble et le style de chaque attraction.*

(source not known)

Backstage posing with LES CHARLIVEL

Valentino, Juanito, and Charles, sons of the famous Spanish clown Charlie Rivel.

We do not see them [Laurel and Hardy] again at the end of *Made in Paris*, floor show a frenzied pace with Daisy Daix is the beautiful and vibrant star and with each number achieves a kind of perfection: exquisite distinction of Florence and Frédérique, who join the strength of the romantic-style acrobatics dancing, comedy dancing duo of Fokkers; surprising Charlivel we do not know if they are more than stunt dancers or musicians, alternating arrangements of Chopin and triple somersaults, sets of swirls and twirls solos maddening, exquisite grace of Mears Felton Girls of models and dancers alternate from an amorous party in Versailles to a Brazilian Carnival ... A show that, to a presentation between everything refined and luxurious, joined these top-class qualities, the pace of the set and the style of each attraction.

## STANLEY! WE HAVE VISITORS

Internationally known Spanish circus clown Charlie Rivel, himself, paying a visit, backstage at the Lido.'

Rivel in his younger days, with his much younger sons.

LEFT: France's top comedy actor Fernandel. — RIGHT: Rene Fraday, co-producer of the Lido Revue.

Members of the St. Etienne Football Club, who have come to watch the best team in the world.
[I hope to goodness not all of these are football players.]

Barely had Laurel and Hardy commenced their season at the Lido when they had to take time out to make a guest appearance at a huge benefit show, staged to raise funds for the Red Cross:

**SPORTS PALACE**

Monday, November 10

From 9pm till dawn

**BIG NIGHT OF THE RED CROSS**

With an appearance by

**LAUREL and HARDY**

by permission of the LIDO

and Marie Bizet – BOURVIL

André DASSARY – Luis MARIANO

**GRAND NIGHT BALL**

One source commented:

*Les deux célèbres comiques Américains Laurel et Hardy occupent depuis quelques jours l'affiche d'un grand cabaret des Champs-Elysees où ils remportent un vif succes.*

The two famous American comedians [*sic*] Laurel and Hardy have been busy for a few days doing a big cabaret show on the Champs-Elysees, where they were a huge success.

Confusion exists as to whether Stan and Babe did their act, at the Lido, in French or English. The French magazine *Image du Monde* printed an abridged version of the script, in French, with the caption:

Laurel & Hardy perform this sketch every night. They don't know what they're saying, because they don't understand a word of French.

Stan and Babe's command of French was VERY limited – limited, in fact, to quoting the odd phrase or two in French. Interjecting a tiny number of French phrases into spoken English would hardly make the patter understandable to non-English speakers, so I would question if they actually continued with that arrangement for the full duration of the six-week run. In the only known photograph of Laurel & Hardy actually performing on stage [See right!] there does not appear to be any props or scenery, and no sign of "the cop." In fact, the two comedians are working on a small area next to the Tony Proteau Orchestra which, in all probability, was the dance floor, used by guests after the show.

Doing their pre-sketch cross-patter, next to the orchestra

Based on that photo, and factoring in that most of the audience members could not understand the patter, I would be willing speculate that, following a few nights of trying to put across the full version of *The Driver's Licence* sketch, with its twelve minutes of wordplay, and getting little-to-no response from the multi-national audience, Stan and Babe decided to do the much shortened two-handed version of the sketch, which they had used so effectively on the US Tours between 1940 and 1942.

The part of Laurel & Hardy's act which gave audiences the greatest thrill, was just in seeing them walk out on stage, and then taking time to acquaint oneself that this really was *them* – the two characters they had seen in those classic comedy films. The novelty of the act was the song and dance routines which they ended on, so what came in the middle was a bonus which, as such, did not need to last too long.

One must also question if Laurel & Hardy were needed to attract people to the Lido. The Lido's main asset is not the appearance of comics, not even French comics, but is the floor show, which can fill the venue on its own merit. So a much shortened, almost token, appearance could well have satisfied the management, guests, and artistes alike. However, that remains my supposition – until such time as a contemporary report contradicts me.

Whatever version of the sketch was enacted, Laurel remained unhappy with the Lido as a venue in which to perform their act. Although by no means a prudish man in real life, Laurel was always protective of the act, which he fastidiously worked on to keep suitable for children. In 1961 when he received an Honorary Academy Award for "services to film comedy" he christened his Oscar statuette "Mr. Clean." Many fans believe that he gave it this nickname because he was always polishing it – which isn't the case at all. He called it "Mr. Clean" because it was testament to the one hundred and sixty-plus films he had appeared in containing no smut, or sexual content. Here though, in the twilight of his stage career, he had to come to terms with performing the act in the middle of a revue show, the main content of which was scantily clad, and even topless, showgirls – thus breaking his unwritten rule of their shows always being suitable for children.

If Laurel regarded the entertainment at the Lido as merely a "flesh" show – the likes of which he would have seen in burlesque, and the kind that Britain was to see in the late-fifties and early-sixties – then he was doing it a dis-service. As already outlined, there **was** much flesh on display at the Lido, but the class of presentation – with its beautiful girls, stunning costumes, spectacular scenery, stirring music, and fabulous dance routines – raised it to an art form. The girls are chosen under strict guidelines, mainly regarding bodily shape and size, from which the resultant selection is a chorus-line of almost identical-looking bodies. In this way, it does not attract the lower element of audience observation, as gone is the element of comparing the sizes of certain favourite parts of the female anatomy Thus, audiences of men and women alike are able to accept the spectacle as pure beauty in symmetry.

The Lido's lead leggy dancer Daisy Daix

46

The former is my opinion, but does not change Laurel's opinion, as he remained unhappy throughout the run at the Lido, and regarded their part of the show as a flop. One has to accept that their show *did* exclude children, and that the act would have achieved nothing like the huge laughs it received when performed in front of an all-English speaking audience, in theatre-style seating, but a flop – no!

Stan's feelings of woe were not just confined to the situation in the Lido as, by a horrendous stroke of bad luck, the visitors had arrived back in Paris at the beginning of "the great strike." Riots were frequent and, at times, the Laurels and the Hardys were in fear of being caught up in the violence. The mains services became inoperative, and made their stay at the *George V Hotel* an uncomfortable one. Come the end of the painful six-week run, the touring party were in a dilemma as to how to get out of the French capital, as the transport system was at a virtual standstill. In the end, a coach was hired to ship them secretly out of France, in the middle of the night, and into Belgium. They may well have enjoyed savouring some of the French culture, and observing some of her entertainers at work, but there would be no choruses of *Je ne Regrette Rien* being sung on the coach as it crossed the French-Belgian border.

CHAPTER 8

## THE THEATRE OF DREAMS

The coach the Laurel & Hardy Touring Company had hired to transport them from Paris to Brussels dropped them off at five-o-clock, on the afternoon of Monday 9th December, outside the Alhambra Theatre. Pre-publicity had informed locals that the two comedians would be arriving at THREE o'clock, but still there was a sizable number of them there, these two hours later.

After negotiating their way through the fans *outside*, the Laurel and Hardy party had a barrier of bodies to overcome *inside*, as the foyer was packed with guests and photographers.

Then came the official welcoming committee, among whom were theatre director Paul Van Stalle and comic actor Marcel Roele – the joint writers of the Laurel & Hardy show, *Hollywood Parade*. Also in attendance was Belgian songstress Simone Max, who presented Ida Laurel and Lucille Hardy with a beautiful bouquet of flowers each.

Stan (centre) followed by Ida, and Paul Van Stalle, entering the foyer of the Alhambra.

Paul Van Stalle, Mrs. Button, Hardy, Simone Max, Lucille, Marcel Roele, Laurel, Ida.

The entourage were then led around the back of the auditorium, and into the manager's office, with photographs being taken along the way.

Mrs. Button, Hardy, Harry Moreny, Lucille, Paul Van Stalle, Ida, Mrs. Van Stalle, Laurel, Marcel Roele

Next stop was the stage area, where Stan took time out to entertain the assembly, by tickling the ivories of the grand piano, on stage.

Stan's hands are dirty, so he's playing just the black notes.

But there was no press conference. Anyone trying to strike up an interview was told that the two stars were too tired after all their travelling, but would answer any questions at the press conference being held the following day.

True to their word, Stan and Babe were back at the Alhambra, Tuesday after-noon, for the press conference, held in the theatre bar.

Here are just some of the comments milked from them.

*Les deux grandes vedettes sont bien sympathiques et que la réception qu'elles font, aux délègues de Presse, est empreinte de grande cordialité.*

*Jamais personnalité politique n'a mobilisé plus de journalistes, plus de photographes!*

The two superstars are friendly and the reception they hold, for members of the Press, is imbued with great cordiality.

No politician has ever mobilized more journalists, more photographers!

One reporter asks Laurel:

*Etes-vous déjà venu en Belgique?*

*«Oui, en 1912, au Palace, a Liège, dans une troupe de comiques qui s'appelait: «Les Huit Comiques. J'étais tellement mauvais que je n'ai jouet qu'un seul soir. On a résilie mon contrat le lendemain.*

*On me reverra au même établissement, avec Oliver le 7 janvier prochaine. J'ose espérer que j'aura meilleur accueil. »*

Have you been to Belgium before?

"Yes, in 1912, at the Palace, in Liège, in a comedy troupe which was called 'The Eight Comiques.' I was so bad that I did only one night. They cancelled my contract the next day.

I will be back again at the same venue, with Oliver on January 7 next [1948]. I hope I will be better received."

Stan adds:

*«Il nous est d'ailleurs impossible de sortir ensemble, Oliver et moi, sans être tout de suite reconnus et sans provoquer des rassemblements. Ah! La popularité ! C'est très flatteur, très gentil, mais c'est parfois bien ennuyeux.»*

"It is also impossible for us to go out together, Oliver and me, without being recognized right away and without causing gatherings. Ah! Popularity! It's very flattering, very nice, but it is sometimes very annoying." (Fernand SERVAIS)

During the gathering …

*MM. Van Stalle père et fils, Mme. Oscar Van Stalle font les présentations. Et comme Laurel, Hardy et leur compagnie – dont M. Moreny leur partenaire dans le sketch qu'ils vont jouer — ne parlent que l'anglais, Mme Bouton, femme de l'administrateur de l'établissement, fait office.*

The Hardys and the Laurels with Mrs. Button.

MM. Van Stall father and son, and Mrs. Oscar Van Stall make presentations. As Laurel and Hardy and their company – of which Mr. Moreny is their partner in the sketch they are going to play – speak only English, Ms. Button, wife of the venue's Administrator, takes charge.

One revelation came from the French newspaper *Le Soir* (*The Evening*):

> *Les ménages Laurel et Hardy, accompagnés de leurs domestiques et de leur manager, personnage affable, agité, dont la chevelure blanche et embroussaillée rappelle celle d'Einstein, font leur petit tour d'Europe. Voyage d'agrément avant tout, parait-il. Mais il s'agirait de s'entendre sur la signification du mot agrément. Le plaisir de toucher de robustes cachets doit y être inclus.*

Laurel and Hardy and their wives are on a little tour of Europe, accompanied by their servants and their manager, a fair-spoken nervous person whose white and bushy hair reminds one of Einstein. A pleasure trip before all, so it seems. But it's all about what you understand by pleasure. The pleasure of getting a hearty fee must be included.

By the description: "a fair-spoken nervous person whose white and bushy hair reminds one of Einstein," I surmise that the reporter is identifying not the manager of the European section of Laurel and Hardy's tour, but their attorney/business manager, Ben Shipman, who must have travelled over from Los Angeles to be at the opening.

Ben Shipman – Laurel and Hardy's attorney-manager. Or is it Einstein?

It was noted that, throughout the two-hour conference, champagne and whisky flowed liberally – encouraging confidence and camaraderie between the assembled guests. That's my Boys!

This was Stan and Babe's second media interview of the day. That morning, they had been interviewees on a radio show at the Institut National de Radiodiffusion (INR), housed in the National Belgian Radio Building, situated in the Place Flagey, in Brussels.

Arriving at the National Belgian Radio Building.

The interview was recorded onto a disc, as magnetic-strip audio recordings were not available at that time. It lasts less than three minutes, which is a bit of a relief – as it makes for uncomfortable listening. The Dutch inter-viewer struggles not only with his English, but with posing questions to which Stan and Babe can give interesting answers. Stan tries to contribute by speaking French, but then totally dries up after one sentence in which, ironically, he apologises for not being able to speak French. He does inject some humour when he tells of being thrown out of Liège in 1912 [when playing a sketch at the Place Theatre, as part of the troupe 'The 8 Comiques']. He follows up this brief anecdote up by wisecracking that, when he and Hardy play Liège in a few weeks' time, he will probably be thrown out again. Strangely, he changed the wording of this story for a less humorous version at the afternoon press conference.

While Hardy (whom the interviewer constantly addresses as Mr. Harley) is talking about their arrival in Belgium the previous day, his wife Lucille prompts him into telling what happened at customs. "Oh yes!" Hardy says, "we came right through. They only held us up for four hours." At which Laurel interjects: "That was for signing pictures."

Laurel wasn't joking. A newspaper article backs up what happened at the France-Belgium border: "Yesterday, instead of searching Laurel and Hardy's two tons of luggage, the customs officers cheered them and asked for autographs."

The highlight of the interview is a couple of instances were Laurel manages to overcome the mundaneness of it all, and breaks into that wonderful real-life laugh of his.

Also in the INR building were the Boyd Bachman Orchestra, who were there to play on-air music. Boyd Bachman(n) was a Dane, but his orchestra was made up of Dutch musicians. They were a show-band really, performing comedy between musical numbers. One comedy interlude in their repertoire was a Laurel & Hardy sketch, performed by orchestra members Henk van Stiphout and Jacques van Wouw.

Back row, middle: Jacques van Wouw (with trombone) [Laurel].
Boyd Bachman is standing between Babe and Stan.
First row standing, second from right (next to Laurel), is Henk van Stiphout (with moustache) [Hardy].
Seated front row centre is Lou van Rees (with sax).

INR Studios luncheon, Brussels. 10 December 1947.

With their mutual love of music AND comedy, the boys of the band and the Boys of Hollywoodland were soon clowning around together. Not wanting to leave the band's company, Stan and Babe invited Bach and his boys to join them at the luncheon, laid on by the radio institution, within the building. Whether or not the BBO had to play music during the luncheon has not been confirmed; but, either way, they would have been thrilled to be in the company of their comedy heroes.

On the top table: Lucille and Oliver Hardy, Ida and Stan Laurel. Seated in front of the Hardys is Harry Moreny (*ibid*). Standing at the back is the Boyd Bachman Orchestra, with Bachman himself between Babe and Ida. Other band members are Henk van Stiphout, behind Ida; and Jacques van Wouw behind Ollie. (Lou van Rees is missing from the photo).

*I was very proud to meet them both. Norman Wisdom*

Stan and Babe were to meet Norman Wisdom on future British Tours. This photo was taken backstage at the Prince of Wales Theatre, London. (6th October 1952)
Inscription reads: *I was very proud to meet them both. Norman Wisdom*

Between 10-18th December Stan and Babe spent time rehearsing at the Alhambra. The show playing there that week was *Piccadilly Nights*, which featured English variety acts, among whom was diminutive comedian Norman Wisdom. Stan and Babe had shared the stage with Norman for a one-night charity show, *The Rats Revel,* at the Victoria Palace, London, back in April.

One of Norman's spots in the current show was a paper-hanging sketch. One night his partner in the sketch slipped off the ladder, which had become slippery with wallpaper paste, and hurt his ankle. The following day, Stan, who stayed on after rehearsals to chat with Norman before each early-show, immediately volunteered to take over the role. The theatre manager said that Laurel would be recognised, so Stan said he would do it in disguise. Nothing could have thrilled Norman more than the thought of working with his idol, but it only served to horrify the theatre Director, Paul Van Stall, who wasn't going to risk his following week's headliner getting injured.

[AJM: For anyone who wishes to visualise what Stan's part in the sketch would have been, you need only get hold of a copy of the 1961 *Sunday Night at the London Palladium* television special, in which Norman performed the said sketch with Bruce Forsyth.]

Working the Alhambra was going to prove a whole lot different to playing the Lido de Paris. The latter was a revue bar, on one level, with guests distributed around tables, and distracted by meals and drinks being served, then cleared; and vision restricted by clouds of smoke, unable to rise because of the low ceiling. At the Alhambra, though, all the audience would be in tiered-seating, facing the stage; and missing would be the constant human traffic. And here, the stage would be a huge, raised platform, which could accommodate all the props, furniture and scenery used in the presentation of their sketch. Gone too would be the resident revue of nubile ladies, and in their place a variety of support acts. Yes, indeed, Laurel and Hardy were going to enjoy their stay at the Alhambra

They were also to enjoy the luxurious surroundings and eloquent service of the Metropole Hotel where, unlike in their hotel in Paris, the plumbing, laundry service, and electrics were fully functional.

[The Alhambra Theatre (seating capacity 2,500), located at the Boulevard Emile Jacqmain, was an important venue in the cultural life of Brussels (Bruxelles) between 1846 and 1974. It was mainly a drama theatre but did, in later times, switch between Variety, Revue, and Operetta.]

The Laurel and Hardy show, billed as *Hollywood Parade* (even though they were the only Hollywood act in it) commenced at the Alhambra Theatre on 19th December, and was to play twice-daily (4:30pm and 8pm) for two weeks – ending 1st January 1948.

Rehearsing, on stage at the Alhambra.

Normally, the first write-up is a review of the show *after* the newspaper critic has seen it. However, this particular journalist chose to do a write-up of an interview with Laurel and Hardy – *before* the show:

*Vijf minuten bij Oliver Hardy en Stan Laurel*

*Mister Hardy, in de film zo donderend, wiens haan altijd koning moet kraaien, is in de werkelijkheid een zeer zacht mens. Met zachte stem, een nuance van tederheid daarin, stelt hij zijn echtgenote voor een eenvoudige goedaardige dame die in de kleine loge aan een nog kleiner tafel een stapeltje kerstkaarten zit te schrijven.*

*Laat Oliver zich minder graag uit over zijn bevindingen in Frankrijk, "Denmark and Belgium are tops" zegt hij, daar was I opperbest en een pracht van een publiek.*

*We merken op dat het na al die menigte films die ze reeds hebben gemaakt wel moeilijk moet vallen om nog nieuwe gags en zo uit te denken. Hardy deelt echter die mening niet. "Het komt er op aan", zo laat hij horen, "een passend verhaal te vinden. De gags spruiten er dan als vanzelf uit voort. Gags op hun eigen hebben niet veel zin. Ze moeten hun bestaansreden putten uit de vertelling."*

*Als de tournée in België is afgelopen, keren Hardy en Laurel naar Hollywood terug. Voor een nieuwe film. Daarna zullen ze een film in Italie draaien.*

*Men zou graag voort keuvelen met een zo aangenaam iemand als Oliver Hardy, maar reeds komt de impressario meedelen dat we ons moeten spoeden, willen we nog een glimp van Stan Laurel opvangen.*

*"Merry Christmas" wensen ons Mister en Mrs Hardy bij het afscheid en op onze beurt wensen we hun een zalig kerst feest toe.*

*Stan Laurel, in zijn hemdsmouwen, heeft haast om gedaan te maken met een ganse reeks fotos waaronder hij zijn handtekening moet zetten.*

*Hij draagt daarbij een bril, de eerste keer dat we zulks van Laurel zien.*

*Zijn streuvelig haar glanst helemaal grijs, zijn kaken zijn nog meer ingevallen dan dat in de film het geval is. Net als hij Hardy is het gelaat verwoest door jaren schmink, maar alle spieren er van gehoorzamen aan de minste druk van de wil.*

*"Mijn beste film ? Fra Diavolo" zegt Stan zonder aarzelen, onderwijl hij naar zijn legendarisch bolhoedje met de smalle randen grijpt en dat zodanig indrukt dat er geen vorm meer aan te bekennen valt. "Een eigenaardig ding, ge kunt het onder een auto gooien, het komt er telkens weer ongehavend onder uit a Tits ! Met duim en wijsvinger heeft Laurel het hoedje de hoogte in gezonden, het valt neer op zijn kop. Een echt werkstukje à la Laurel, we hebben 't hem al tientallen keren zien doen en toch verbaast ons alweer de vlugheid waarmee het gebeurt. We lachen.*

*In de zaal wacht het publiek in spanning het moment af waarop de vermaardste humoristen ter wereld vóór het voetlicht zullen verschijnen. Het laatste nummer, de clou van de avond.*

*Als we de artisten uitgang van de schouwburg bereikten, stellen we vast niet te hebben gezien of Oliver Hardy een snorretje droeg.*

(*Het Volk* – 20th December 1947)

-----0-----

## TRANSLATION (by Bram Reijnhoudt)

### Five Minutes with Oliver Hardy and Stan Laurel

Mister Hardy, in the films such a dominant character, who always has to be cock of the yard is, in reality, a very gentle man. With a soft voice, a nuance of tenderness therein, he introduces his spouse, a simple kind-hearted lady who's writing a stack of Christmas cards in the small dressing-room at an even smaller table.

Less inclined to dwell on his experiences in France, "Denmark and Belgium are tops" he says, the best of all, and wonderful audiences.

We remark that it must be difficult to think of new gags and material after the huge number of films they have already made. But Hardy doesn't share this opinion. "What matters," he informs us, "is to find an appropriate story. The gags will grow from there as a matter of course. Gags on themselves don't make much sense. They have to draw their right of existence from the story telling".

When the tour in Belgium is finished, Hardy and Laurel will return to Hollywood for a new film. Later they will shoot a film in Italy.

One would gladly keep chatting with a man as pleasant as Oliver Hardy, but already the agent turns up to announce that we have to hurry if we still want to catch a glimpse of Stan Laurel.

"Merry Christmas", is Mister and Mrs Hardy's wish when we take our leave and we, on our part, wish them a blessed yuletide.

Stan Laurel, in his shirtsleeves, is in a hurry to finish an entire series of photos that he has to sign. He uses glasses for this, the first time that we have seen them on Laurel.

His straight hair shines all grey, his jaws are even more sunken than is the case in the films. Just as with Hardy, the face is devastated by years of make-up, but all the muscles in him obey to the slightest pressure of his will.

"My best film? Fra Diavolo," says Stan without hesitation, as he grabs his legendary bowler with the small brim and starts pushing it in, till there's no recognizable shape anymore. "A peculiar thing, you can throw it under a car, it emerges every time undamaged." Swat! With thumb and finger Laurel has sent his small hat in the air, it falls on his head. A real routine à la Stan Laurel, we have seen him do it dozens of times and yet we are surprised by the nimbleness with which it happens. We laugh.

In the auditorium the audience are anxiously awaiting the moment when the most famous comedians in the world will appear in front of the footlights. The last number, the main event of the evening.

When we reach the backstage door of the theatre, we can't decide if Oliver Hardy was wearing a moustache.

(Flemish paper *The People* – 20th December 1947)

So that's what was said *before* the show, but what was reported *afterwards*?

CHAPTER 9

## IT'S SHOWTIME!

The reviews at the Brussels Alhambra were from good to jubilant without exception:

### A l'Alhambra Hollywood Parade

*Stan Laurel et Oliver Hardy sont à l'Alhambra en chair et en os, mais il faudra attendre jusqu'au milieu du second acte pour les voir paraître en scène. Chose curieuse cependant, les numéros présentés au cours du premier acte et au début du second sont d'une telle qualité que jamais l'intérêt du présent ne se perd dans l'attente des vedettes du cinéma américain.*

*En somme, l'Alhambra nous présente une revue de la meilleure veine, avec ses ballets parfaitement réglés, ses drôleries bien enlevées, ses numéros de chant de premier choix, ses danses acrobatiques extraordinaires et l'imitateur inimitable Maxim Herman-Raft. Le tout est souligné de la façon la plus heureuse par une excellente partition dont de nombreux thèmes sont dus à la plume de M. Emile Maetens qui dirige magistralement son orchestre.*

*Un choix serait difficile parmi la série d'artistes qui se produisent au cours de ces diverses scènes. Une mention spéciale pourtant à la danseuse acrobatique Mme Betty Gromer, à l'imitateur que nous avons cité plus haut et à l'excellent chanteur Zbiniew Krukowski. Ceci n'implique d'ailleurs nul démérite chez les autres qui, tous, remplissent parfaitement le rôle qui leur est confié.*

*Et voici Laurel et Hardy avec leur suite de gags désopilants, leur contraste hilarant de physionomies, l'imbroglio des malheurs qui pleuvent sur leur tête et qu'ils attirent comme des paratonnerres attirent la foudre. Dès leurs entrée en scène, on rit parce qu'on sait que Laurel et Hardy sont comiques et ce rire de confiance du début entraîne infailliblement les éclats de rire suivants, dès qu'un des deux comiques américains esquisse une chanson, un pas de danse ou une des mimiques qui ont fait leur célébrité. Les gags les plus usés de Laurel et Hardy au cinéma retrouvent toute leur saveur et toute leur fraîcheur à la scène; aussi les applaudissements éclatent-ils unanimes à la fin de chaque numéro. Les deux artistes d'Hollywood ne parlent pas un mot de français. Qu'à cela ne tienne, leurs drôleries ne viennent pas du texte qu'ils débitent, mais de la façon dont ils tirent parti des situations clownesques dans lesquelles ils se fourrent invariablement. Cela plaît incontestablement au public et le succès de cette revue en parait assuré.*

(*La Libre Belgique* – 20th December 1947)

Programme cover

## At the Alhambra Hollywood Parade

Stan Laurel and Oliver Hardy are at the Alhambra, as large as life, but you have to wait until the middle of the second act to see them appear on stage. Nevertheless, the numbers that are presented in the first act, and in the beginning of the second, are of such a high standard that the interest in what is shown doesn't get lost in the expectation of the two stars of American cinema.

All-in-all, the Alhambra offers us a variety show in the best tradition, with its perfectly staged dances, its brightly played jokes, its first class musical numbers, its extraordinary acrobatic dances and the inimitable imitator Maxim Herman-Raft. Everything is stressed in the most happy way by an excellent music score whose many themes come from the pen of M. Emile Maetens who conducts his orchestra brilliantly.

MAXIM HERMAN RAFT
DANS
"HOLLYWOOD PARADE"
AVEC
STAN LAUREL & OLIVER HARDY

It would be difficult to make a choice between all the artists who appear during the different scenes. A special note however for acrobatic dancer Miss Betty Gromer, for the above-mentioned impersonator and for the excellent singer Zbiniew Krukowski. This doesn't implicate any shortcomings with the others who, all of them, perfectly fulfill the part that was entrusted to them.

And then we have Laurel and Hardy with their succession of hilarious gags, their hilarious contrasting physiognomy, the muddle of accidents which rains down on them, and which they attract like a lightning rod attracts a bolt of lightning. From the moment they enter the stage, one laughs because one knows that Laurel and Hardy are funny and that laughter of confidence in the beginning leads without fail towards later bursts of laughter, as soon as one of the two American comedians only [hints] a song, a little dance or one of their funny faces that made them famous. The gags that Laurel and Hardy most often used in the films regain on stage all of their flavour and all of their freshness; at the end of each gag the unanimous applause explodes. The two artists from Hollywood don't speak a word of French. It does not matter, their funniness doesn't come from the text they are uttering, but from the way they take advantage of the farcical situations in which they invariably get into. The audience undisputably loved this and the success of this revue seems assured.

(*La Libre Belgique* – 20th December 1947)

*La Dernière Heure* (21st December 1947) confirmed the Hollywood stars' reception:

*Enfin il y a Laurel et Hardy. Leur apparition fut saluée par un tonnerre d'applaudissements qui se renouvéla, amplifié encore, lorsqu'ils vinrent saluer le public après leur numéro. C'est que tous deux furent bien tels qu'on les attendait: bons enfants, ahuris, cocasses. On aurait pu craindre que, privés des truquages du cinéma, leur comique eût été moins efficace. Il n'en est rien. Leur "présence" sur scène est incomparable et si les moyens qu'ils emploient sont forcément usés, ils n'en atteignent pas moins leur but. Ce sont de très grands artistes.*

-----0-----

Finally there is Laurel and Hardy. Their appearance was greeted by a thunder of applause which renewed itself, even stronger, when they saluted the public after their act. Both men were exactly what everyone expected them to be: innocent children, dimwits, funny. One could have believed that, without the special effects of the films, their funny side would be less effective. Nothing of the sort. Their "presence" on stage is incomparable and even if the means they are employing are used over and over again, they don't fail to reach their goal. They are very great artists.

But, not forgetting the contribution of the support acts:

*Les décors et les costumes de cette revue sont de toute beauté. Et sans Laurel et Hardy, on irait encore à l'Alhambra pour le beau chanteur qu'est Zbiniew Krubowski. pour le film historique muet où se produisent Billy-Pitt, Guy-Lou Sassoye, Jannelin et Rosie Darvil; pour les imitations de l' "inimitable" Maxim Herman-Raft, le bien nommé, pour une étonnante danseuse acrobatique, Betty Gromer, et pour bien d'autres choses encore, parmi lesquelles il nous plait d'inscrire l'adaptation musicale d'Emile Maetens, animateur de classe.*

-----0-----

The sets and costumes for this review are beautiful. Without Laurel and Hardy, one would still go to the Alhambra for the beautiful singer who is Zbiniew Krubowski, for the silent historical film in which Billy Pitt, Guy-Lou Sassoye, Jannelin Darvil and Rosie appear; for the imitations by the "inimitable" Maxim Herman-Raft, aptly named; for an amazing acrobatic dancer, Betty Gromer; and for many other things, among which we would like to include the musical adaptation by Emile Maetens, a class host.

Thought to be two of the support acts from "Hollywood Parade".

A fourth review told us more about Laurel and Hardy's sketch:

*Laurel et Hardy passent au milieu du second acte et leur sketch "Permis de conduire" dure un bon quart d'heure.*

*La tempête de bravos qui acceuille leur entrée en scène se renouvelle à leur sortie – et cela suffit à signaler que leur succès n'est pas seulement un succès de curiosité...Sans doute, les disponibilités inépuisables du cinéma permettent-els à ces clowns de grande classe de trouvailles d'une énormité que ne peut produire le théâtre. Mais leur présence, en chair et en os, soulève une sympathie plus directe et plus démonstrative de la part du public. Ceci compense cela.*

*Laurel, Hardy – et leur bon partenaire Jacques Henley – s'expriment en anglais; mais leurs "effets" sont avant tout visuels, ce qui ne déçoit guère les spectateurs peu familiarisés avec cette langue. Ce qui compte, c'est à dire, ce qui fait s'esclaffer, dans cette quelconque histoire de deux apprentis chauffeurs aux prises avec le policier qui délivre des certificats de compétence, ce sont des loufoqueries occassionelles, qui n'ont aucun rapport avec l'histoire elle-même: le pansement que Laurel porte à son doigt blessé et dont il tirera parti tout le long du sketch, le pied endolori de Hardy, que celui-ci évente gracieusement (?) avec un chapeau; les chapeaus des deux compères et le képi du policier, qu'ils se disputent tous les trois dans une ahurissante colère; les paperasses du commissariat que Hardy et Laurel lancent en l'air dans un sursaut d'effroi après les avoir étagées soigneusement sur un coin du bureau...toutes ces bouffonneries indescriptibles sont pour les deux grands comiques autant de "gags" dont on a honte de rire, mais qui font rire irrésistiblement, sans répit, durant quinze bonnes, quinze folles minutes.*

(*Le Soir* – 21st December 1947)

Laurel and Hardy appear in the middle of the second act and their sketch "The Driver's Licence" lasts a good quarter of an hour. The storm of cheers with which they are greeted when entering the stage repeats itself when leaving it – enough to indicate that their success is not only a success of curiosity...No doubt, the inexhaustible availabilities of the cinema allow these two first class clowns to use ingenious finds that cannot be produced in the theatre. But their presence, in the flesh, raises a more direct and more demonstrative friendship from the audience. It makes up for that.

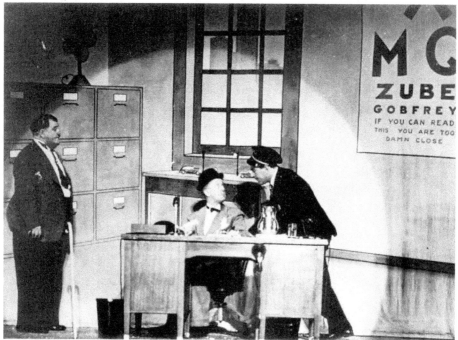

Jacques Henley as 'the cop' in "The Driver's Licence" sketch

Laurel, Hardy – and their good partner Jacques Henley – express themselves in English; but their "effects" are, above all, visual – and it hardly disapoints the spectators who are not familiar with this language. What counts is, that is, what makes you burst out laughing in this little story of two apprentice drivers battling against a policeman who shows great signs of skill, is the occasional craziness that has nothing to do with the story itself: the bandage that Laurel wears around his injured finger and that he takes advantage of during the whole sketch, Hardy's painful foot that he fans gracefully with his hat; the hats of our two friends and the policeman that they fight over in a stupefying fury; the paperwork of the police station that they throw in the air in a sudden burst of fright after having them carefully arranged on a corner of the desk ... all this indescribable buffoonery are for the two great comics as much gags that one is ashamed of to laugh with, but make you laugh irresistably and continuously during fifteen good and crazy minutes...

-----0-----

Further credit was given to the following:

*MM. Paul Van Stalle et Marcel Roele, auteurs de Hollywood Parade, ont prouvé, une fois de plus leur savoir-faire. Nul doute que le public bruxellois ne se précipite à l'Alhambra, pour voir et entendre Laurel et Hardy, "en chair et en os" présentés par ces maîtres en présentation. Jacques Henley donnant la réplique.*

MM. Paul Van Stalle and Marcel Roele, writers of *Hollywood Parade*, have proved once again their expertise. No doubt the Brussels' public will rush to the Alhambra, to see and hear Laurel and Hardy, "in the flesh" presented by these masters of stagecraft. Jacques Henley is the foil.

As Jacques Henley is again billed as assisting Laurel & Hardy (as 'the cop' in *The Driving Licence* sketch) it leaves one to ask in what capacity Harry Moreny was being retained – if at all.

The proceeds from the opening night of the show were donated to a military charity, as outlined below:

*Cette première des deux comiques américains était un gala organisé par les Fraternelle 1914-18 et 1940-45 du 12e de ligne au profit de leurs caisses de secours.*

*Les anciens du régiment qui se distingua parmi tous les autres au cours des deux guerres avaient répondu nombreux a l'appel des membres de leurs comités, et la salle était fort bien garnie.*

-----0-----

This premiere of the show by the two American comics was a gala hosted by the Fraternity 1914-18 and 1940-45 12th line for the benefit of their relief funds.

The veterans of the regiment, which distinguished itself among all others during two wars, had responded in number to the call of the members of their committees, and the room was packed.

There were many high-ranking officials in attendance, including the military attaché from the United States Embassy, and all paid due respect to those who had fought for the allies.

It was a very generous gesture by Stan and Babe, and the management of the Alhambra, to donate the proceeds to the military charity – but this was only a half of their generosity, as the proceeds of the matinée show had also been donated. This facsimile of the newspaper advert will explain all:

| | |
|---|---|
| C'est le vendredi 19 décembre à 16h 30 que vous irez applaudir au THEATRE DE L'ALHAMBRA Vos deux vedettes préférés **LAUREL ET HARDY** Cette représentation, qui est la première de la Grande Revue dans laquelle se produiront les célèbres comiques, est donnée au profit des ENFANTS DE LA PATRIE Le spectacle pouvant être vu par tous, ne manquez pas d'y conduire vos enfants, les associant ainsi à une magnifique oeuvre de charité. | It is this Friday December 19th at 4.30 pm that you are going to applaud your two favourite stars at the ALHAMBRA THEATRE **LAUREL AND HARDY** This performance, which is the the premiere of the Great Revue in which the famous comedians will appear on stage, is given for the benefit of the CHILDREN OF THE HOMELAND. The show is suited for everyone, don't forget to bring your children, thus including them in a wonderful act of charity. |

The newspaper *La Dernière Heure* (The Last Hour) explained the aims of the charity:

*Parents! Conduisez vos enfants à cette matinée extraordinaire, donnée en faveur des*

***ENFANTS DE LA PATRIE***

*Ce sera pour eux la plus belle récompense de fin d'année de pouvoir à la fois applaudir leurs vedettes favorites et d'accomplir un magnifique geste de solidarité envers les petits malheureux dont le père a donné sa vie pour la patrie.*

-----0-----

Parents! Bring your children to this extraordinary matinee given for the benefit of the CHILDREN OF THE HOMELAND

For them it will be the most beautiful New Year's gift to, at the same time, be able to applaud their favourite stars and to accomplish a wonderful gesture of solidarity towards those unfortunate children whose father gave his life for his country.

One evening (or more), during Laurel and Hardy's three-week stay in Brussels, Stan took his wife Ida to a cabaret restaurant – named "Chez Harry Dressel" ("Harry Dressel's Place") – located at Bishops Street 26, Rue dee l'Evêque.

Paul van Stalle; Mrs. Thys; Stan,
Harry Dressel (standing)
Ida Laurel; Mrs. Martens; and
Mr. Martens (Musical Director)
Rosie Darvil (English singer from
*Hollywood Parade*)

The owner of the venue was Dutch entertainer Harry Dressel (real name "Dresselhuys"). For his stage act, Harry's character was that of a 'Hollander,' for which he dressed in the Volendammer traditional costume – from his hat down to his white wooden clogs – and cracked jokes about tulips and cheese, and all things Dutch. He decorated the hat with three red balls (which is not authentic dress) and then made comic references about his "three balls."

This may be part of Harry Dressel's regular stage act, in which he gets a couple out of the audience,
and uses them as stooges. In this instance, Mr. & Mrs. Laurel were the "volunteers."
Ida has been given the traditional headwear of the Volendammer costume, the 'hul', to wear; while
Stan is sporting the Volendammer men's hat. (We won't mention the three balls).

RIGHT: Glamorous Hollywood star Jane Seymour modelling the Volendammer costume on a visit to
the museum, rather than a hat which has been battered over the years in Harry Dressel's prop box.

Because of the location of Chez Harry, close to the Alhambra and the Metropole Hotel, it was the chosen eatery for show business acts, as they knew they would not be pestered to the same extent they would in a public restaurant. As a comedy entertainer for nearly two decades, and having worked the Lido de Paris and the Brussels Alhambra, Dressler would have been thrilled to compare notes with Laurel about stage shows.

Why Hardy didn't take up the invite, or how the evening went, isn't known. What happened at *Chez Harry*, stayed at *Chez Harry*.

CHAPTER 10

## ON THE WRONG TRACK

At the end of the two-week run at the Alhambra, which took them into the New Year, Laurel and Hardy were about to embark on a series of two shows a day, around other parts of Belgium. One would think that towns and cities accommodating the Laurel & Hardy Show for just the one day had an easy task but, as Laurel's screen character might well have said, "Don't cross your bridges before they've hatched."

### Friday 2nd January 1948 — ANTWERP (Dutch = Antwerpen. French = Anvers)

The schedule for the Laurel & Hardy Co. was to leave Brussels at 1:15pm, and travel the twenty-eight miles due north to Belgium's second-city (and largest port) Antwerp, to arrive by 2pm. Shows were at 4pm and 9pm. But this was no theatre they were about to play, it was the Sportpaleis (Sports Palace) a vast domed stadium – not designed for listening to two tiny men talking to each other. Picture a huge cafeteria area, seating hundreds of diners. Now surround the seating area with a velodrome (a motorcycle and cycle track). Now surround that track with stands for spectators, similar to the arrangement at motor-racing venues – and that is the setting the Boys were next pitched into.

To put on Laurel and Hardy's stage sketch in a theatre was not difficult, nor anything the like of which hadn't been practised for "hundreds of centuries of generations." All they needed was a stage; a desk for the police officer; and an audience of fans facing the stage. Here, at the Sports Palace, they got none of that.

If Laurel & Hardy had been the sole attraction, then maybe the organisers could have arranged the café seating area so that the diners were facing a small platform where the two comedians could perform at least part of their act. But that wasn't going to happen as not only were the Hollywood stars **not** the main attraction, but they were so far down the bill that (in the words of the old music-hall gag) they were in danger of falling off the poster.

The event was a Sports Gala, to raise money to erect a monument in honour of members of the Belgian police force who had been killed in service during the two World Wars.

Laurel greeting one of the policeman attending the charity show at the Sportspaleis, staged to honour his fallen colleagues.

Stan and Babe were always quick to support worthwhile charities but, on this occasion, they had been *too* quick. Each year the Sportpaleis hosted the immensely popular "Zesdaagse" – a race which lasted <u>six days</u> in a carnival-like atmosphere. Also, as recently as 1945, Belgium had been staging another annual cycle race, the "Omloop Het Volk" (The People Circuit), one of the seven races which constitute "the Classics." Thus, Belgium had a fanatical following of racing fans, thousands of whom were about to turn to up to watch the races at the Sportpaleis – and of which few, if any, gave a hoot about Laurel and Hardy.

At the 4pm show, 5,000 spectators watched various competitive races, and some novelty ones – such as a roller-skating race; a cross-country for policemen; and some comedy business with a clown's car. At the evening show, the numbers of spectators had swelled to a massive 22,000. The majority of these were there to see past champions compete – the most popular of whom was Georges Ronsse (World Cycling Champion in both 1928 and 29).

So what of Laurel and Hardy? How did they survive amid all this action? Well, the answer is that, sorry to say – "they didn't." The reviewer for *De Gentenaar* commented:

> *Zeggen dat ze veel succes hadden met het vertoonde zullen we hoegenaamd noet vooropzetten, vermits het nummertje dat ze gaven veel te kort was.*

> *Met Stan Laurel, een aangename man in den omgang wat niet kan gezegd worden van Oliver Hardy, heb ik enkele minutjes kunnen klappen en hij vond het zeer spijtig dat het vooropgezet nummer – een sketch die vooral toepasselijk was op de politiemannen, waarvoor de meeting was ingericht – niet kon doorgaan vermits de omlijsting ontbrak.*

TRANSLATION

> I had the opportunity to talk to Stan Laurel for a few minutes, an amiable man, which cannot be said of Oliver Hardy, and he very much regretted that the act – a sketch which was particularly suitable for the policemen for whom the meeting had been organised – was cancelled because the surroundings were not appropriate.

From this comment, I would surmise that Stan and Ollie did the first part of their act – the talking bit before they go into *The Driver's Licence* sketch. This would have been the well-used routine in which Hardy makes a speech, saying how wonderful it was to be in [insert name of place], whilst Laurel continuously interrupts him. The pay-off, when Ollie asks Stan what he wants, is Stan delivering the punchline: "You're standing on my foot." Short indeed.

The stewards and track marshals, about to break the news to Laurel and Hardy
that they are going to have to do a bike race. Sportspaleis, Antwerp.

The routine would have had as little an effect on this crowd as a comedian, in ancient Roman times, standing in front of 5,000 spectators who had come to watch a chariot race. So, for the evening show, the two comedians and the organisers would have been fully aware that to attempt any kind of stage presentation would be futile. That is when some bright spark figured that "spectacle" was what was needed, and in such a way that everyone could see Laurel and Hardy "in-the-round." And so "a bike race" between the two comedians was decided upon.

At first, Stan and Babe refused to participate, but pressure from the organisers, and the thought of "getting the bird" from 22,000 paying customers, there to raise money for the war dead, pretty much compelled them to comply.

The view of the two world-famous comedians speeding around the track on cycles, with the crowd whistling, clapping, and cheering them on, was what had been envisaged. But the vision did not last long – not long at all. The race was stopped within the first hundred metres, because of a pile-up which had occurred just before Laurel and Hardy were to do their piece, and which was still obstructing the track.

The Tortoise and the Tortoise
Stewards assisting Stan and Babe to mount their bikes, at the start of the race at the Sportsplaeis, Antwerp. 2nd January 1948.

Life Imitating Art.
Here the Boys can be seen getting around the Hal Roach Lot, during the making of their 1935 film *Bonnie Scotland*.

We know from Stan's earlier confession to a reporter that he and Babe were disappointed the planned sketch could not be performed, but it would have been less painful if the bike race, too, had been cancelled, as the whole event fell flat, and showed the two film comedians in a bad light.

I shan't include the unkind comments they received for their participation at the Gala, but will defend L&H by saying that the hastily improvised cycle race, which was not of their making, was totally ill-advised — especially for two men of their age and physical condition. It should have been obvious beforehand that the Sportpaleis Gala was completely the wrong venue, audience, and setting, in which to introduce the two stage comedians. You might just as well drop a set of snooker balls onto a muddy patch of ground in front of the stage at the Glastonbury Festival, and invite the world's top two snooker players to play a game of snooker, while the music fans are watching the bands on stage. That's how misplaced the idea was.

LAUREL and HARDY – The European Tours

The good news – apart from all the money raised for the police benefit – is that, at least, Laurel and Hardy didn't receive a bashing in the local press. The *Antwerp Gazette* reported only:

DE DAG DER POLITIE

Grote gala in het Sportpaleis

Stan. Laurel en Oliver Hardy zoals wij hen zagen in het Sportpaleis.

Stan. Laurel and Oliver Hardy as we them saw in the sports palace.

Er was ook nog een andere wedstrijd waar Stan Laurel en Olivier Hardy een velokoers op de piste angingen. Ze schenen geen van belden zadelvast te zitten en ten slotte was het Laurel die de koers won.

-----0-----

TRANSLATION

THE DAY FOR THE POLICE

Huge Gala at the Sports Palace

There was also another competition where Stan Laurel and Oliver Hardy came onto the sloping cycle track. Neither seemed very sure in the saddle, and finally it was Laurel who won the race.

And there was even better news:

Na afloop van de voorstelling vangst van de artisten plaats in in het Sportpaleis had een ont een zaal van de middenstad waar de burgemeester Craeybeckx de twee filmvedetten toesprak.

(*Gazet van Antwerpen* – 4th January 1948)

After the performance in the Sports Palace, Mayor Craeybeckx received the artists in a venue in the city-centre, where he made a speech addressing the two film celebrities.

(*Antwerp Gazette* – 4th January 1948)

-----0-----

And here is that very speech:

2<sup>nd</sup> January 1948

Dearest Stan Laurel and Oliver Hardy,

I suppose you don't want us to give this reception the character of an official, dry ceremony. Friends, we are among friends. Therefore allow me to omit the commonplace handle to your names. Everybody may be a Mr.; as for you both, you are for us plain Stan and Oliver.

In a world which is out of square and where to-morrow is a mystery, a jigsaw puzzle, you have found the means of shooing, if only for a few short moments, the fear that darkens the mind, the sorrow that fills the heart, the trouble that breaks energy and makes man infirm of purpose. You have shown us the power of irony, and you have put in practice the great precept that we should be able to laugh away despondency.

Men and women become children again when seeing you, spontaneous laughter bubbles up, and believe me, notwithstanding grandiloquent philosophical erudition and would-be learning, there is the true palliative, nay, the powerful remedy against despair. There is no pose in you, no make believe, no fool-farming. You are the practical philosophers. We may think of the Jitterbugs, of Fre Diavolo [*sic*], of the Legionaries, of Big Noise, of so many other sparkling jewels : each time we discover wit and boisterous joy in features and gestures, treasure-troves with unexpected and irresistible effects.

It is no too much when I say : you are characteristic representatives of a great nation which is in the crucial moments of its history gave such imposing proofs of its vitality.

We dearly hope you will proceed.

Long live optimism Three cheers for Stan Laurel and Oliver Hardy :

Hurrah ! Hurrah ! Hurrah !

-----0----

*Fra Diavolo* (1933) and *Les Deux Legionairies* (1931) are indeed two classic films which Laurel & Hardy made at the Hal Roach studios (the latter being the French release of *Beau Hunks*); but, in naming *Jitterbugs* (1943) and *The Big Noise* (1944) as sparkling jewels, it would appear that the Mayor of Antwerp had seen very few of the vast catalogue of Laurel & Hardy shorts and features pre-1940, as the post-1940 films are poor paste copies only.

Be that as it may, after losing their dignity on the track, the two film legends were leaving with their dignity restored by the Mayor paying his respects. Thankfully, regular stages in regular theatres with regular fans would be all that Laurel and Hardy had to contend with on the rest of this Belgian tour. As for "The Tour de France" – that is one tour Stan and Babe would not be making in the foreseeable future.

[AJM: Sincere thanks to Laurel & Hardy historian and author, Bram Reijnhoudt, for his valued assistance with this Antwerp appearance].

-----0-----

## Saturday 3<sup>rd</sup> January — CHARLEROI

After the Friday night appearance in Antwerp, the Laurels and the Hardys would almost certainly have been driven back to the Metropole Hotel, in Brussels. From there, the next day, they left at 1pm, to make the thirty-eight-mile journey south to Charleroi by 2pm. The two shows at the Théâtre des Variétés were at 2:45 and 7:30 pm.

As Charleroi is the third-biggest city in Belgium, and the biggest city in Wallonia (the French-speaking part of Belgium) one would have expected that, with Laurel and Hardy playing just four shows at the Theatre of Varieties, it would be sold out. But, according to the local newspaper review, that was far from the case:

**De la scène à l'écran – *Laurel et Hardy* au Théâtre des Variétés**

*Quelle qui soit la popularité de Laurel et Hardy, qui étaient samedi et dimanche les hôtes de Charleroi, elle n'a pas suffi pour remplir la salle des "Variétés" lors des représentations données par les deux vedettes de cinéma.*

*C'est donc devant un public assez clairsemé que se déroula la revue "Hollywood Parade" qui n'a d'autre but que d'enchâsser le sketch où triomphent les deux comiques américains.*

*Ce n'est pas que cette revue soit dépourvue de mérite, mais elle sent la facilité et la troupe elle-même contribue par un jeu mécanique, à renforcer cette impression. Le premier tableau, pourtant, ne manque pas d'esprit et évoque de façon burlesque l'agonie du théâtre, supplanté par le cinéma.*

*Le second n'est qu'un prétexte à introduire le tour de chant du baryton Krukowski, qui fait applaudir une voix bien timbrée et d'un beau volume dans l'arioso de Benvenuto Cellini de Diaz.*

*Le public a fort apprécié aussi le dynamisme de Betty Gromer, une danseuse acrobatique qui exécute avec brio et grâce des sauts de carpe, sauts arabes et sauts périlleux sur un pied, qui sont de véritables prouesses.*

*Dans une courte scène comique "Au nom du fisc" Georges Davray se montre un contrôleur de contributions plein de naturel et de bonhomie.*

*Après une scène exotique "Mirage" avec le baryton Krukowski, Maxim Herman-Raft se livre à des imitations de vedettes, dont la moins réussie n'est pas celle de Cheeta, le chimpanzé de Tarzan. Un gros succès aussi est l'imitation de Charlot et celle des voix de Mickey, Donald et Popeye.*

*Une cocasse reconstitution d'un grand film historique du temps du cinéma muet est suivie d'un final animé, au cours duquel se prodiguent dans un ballet de cow-boys et peaux-rouges les "Flower Girls" qui sont plus des "gambilleuses" de revue que de vrais danseuses.*

*Enfin, après deux saynètes musicales, voici, précédés de leur ritournelle devenue fameuse depuis "Laurel et Hardy légionnaires", les deux inséparables de l'écran américain; les voici tels que nous les ont montrés leur désopilantes aventures: Stan Laurel, blème, vieux gamin facétieux (et grisonnant) à la fois impressionnable et désinvolte; Oliver Hardy, luisant, rebondi, énorme et solennel, précieux et susceptible, jaloux de l'autorité tyrannique qu'il exerce sur Laurel (qui se venge parfois cruellement de sa sujétion).*

*Tous les gags auxquels ils nous ont accoutumés, tous leurs tics, nous les reconnaissons avec leurs effets d'hilarité éprouvés par un long visage. Et c'est de les retrouver si pareil à eux-mêmes que le public s'esclaffe. C'est le déferlement de rire quand ils échangent leurs chapeaux, quand Hardy agite sa cravate, quand le visage de Laurel, par de savantes gradations se décompose jusqu'au moment où il fond en larmes sous l'oeil courroucé de son partenaire.*

*Le sketch "Permis de conduire" qu'ils jouent en anglais, n'est qu'une synthèse de tous les jeux de scène et de physionomie qui ont fait leur succès. Et, après des rappels au cours desquels, ils ont l'un et l'autre chanté et dansé (même Hardy avec sa masse impressionnante!) c'est sous les applaudissements nourris qu'ils disparaissent dans les coulisses.*

(*L'Indépendance – Le Quotidien de Charleroi* — 5th January 1948)

-----0-----

### From Stage to Screen – **Laurel and Hardy** at the Théâtre des Variétés

Whatever the popularity of Laurel and Hardy, who were the guests of Charleroi on Saturday and Sunday, may be it was not enough to fill the hall at the "Variétés" during the performances given by the two film stars.

So it was before a rather sparse audience that the revue "Hollywood Parade" took place, which has no other goal than to set the sketch in which the two American comics can shine.

It is not that this revue is deprived of merit, but it feels the easiness and the company itself contributes to reinforce that impression by its artificial playing. The first scene, however, doesn't lack spirit and evokes in a burlesque way the slow death of the theatre, replaced by the cinema.

The second one is just an excuse to introduce the song recital of baritone Krukowski, who gets applause for a nicely toned and volumed voice in the arioso of Benvenuto Cellini by Diaz.

The audience greatly appreciated the dynamics of Betty Gromer, an acrobatic dancer who executes with panache and grace all kinds of jumps and somersaults on one foot that are brilliant achievements.

In a short comical scene "In the Name of Taxes" Georges Davray plays a good-natured tax-inspector.

After an exotic scene "Mirage" with baritone Krukowski, Maxim Herman-Raft delivers impersonations of stars of which the one of Cheeta, Tarzan's chimpanzee, is not the least one. The impersonation of Charlie Chaplin and the imitations of the voices of Mickey Mouse, Donald Duck and Popeye were also a great success.

A funny reconstruction of a historical silent film is followed by a lively finale in which appear lavishly in a dance of cowboys and Red Indians the "Flower Girls," who are more "jigging about" rather than being real dancers.

Getting into character, backstage.

Finally, after two musical playlets, and preceded by their tune that became famous ever since *Beau Hunks*, the two inseparables of the American cinema appear; here they are just as their crazy adventures showed them to us: Stan Laurel, pale, old mischievous kid (and greying), impressionable and casual at the same time; Oliver Hardy, gleaming, chubby, enormous and solemn, precious and touchy, guarding the tyrannical authority he exerts on Laurel (who sometimes cruelly avenges his subjection).

All the gags that they made us familar with, all their twitches [gestures], we recognize them with their hilarious effects, tested on a long face. And it's finding them so similar to themselves that makes the audience burst out laughing. It's the flood of laughter when they swap hats, when Hardy twiddles his tie, when Laurel's face gradually distorts up to the moment that he bursts into tears under the wrathful eye of his partner.

The sketch *The Driver's Licence*, that they are playing in English, is nothing more than a summary of their acting and features [mannerisms] that made their success. And, after a few curtain calls during which they do a song and a dance (even Hardy with his impressive mass!), they vanish into the wings under hearty applause.

-----0-----

It is puzzling as to why *The Laurel & Hardy Revue* failed to attract full-houses in Charleroi. In Brussels, the show had played to packed-houses for two weeks, and there were two additional shows yet to come in early January, to cater for demand; whereas Charleroi had only the four shows to fill seats at. One would have thought that reviews from Brussels had filtered through, or been used in advanced publicity – causing locals to clamour for tickets. The review for the first night was not exactly glowing, but then that should have only affected tickets sales for the *second* night – if at all.

The theatre building had started life in 1910 as a CIRCUS (Le Cirque des Variétés) before being converted to a theatre in 1928. Then in 1935 it had had a major facelift. Maybe it was just what is termed a "White Elephant" – in the sense that it *should* have been successful, but no reason could be given as to why it *wasn't*.

-----0-----

### Sunday 4th January — CHARLEROI

The schedule for the Sunday travel arrangements and shows was the same as for the Saturday, after which, Laurel and Hardy had to move on again. These one- and two-night appearances were killers.

CHAPTER 11

ONE-NIGHTERS

## Monday 5<sup>th</sup> January — VERVIERS

Monday morning at 9:30am found the Laurels and the Hardys leaving Brussels, where they had again stayed the night, giving themselves enough time to make the seventy-eight-mile journey east to Verviers – a Walloon city and municipality located in the Belgian province of Liège, roughly halfway between Liège and the German border.

Upon arrival, they booked in at the Grand Hotel. Shows were at 3:00 and 8:00pm., at the Coliseum Theatre, of which *Le Courrier du Soire* informed us:

*Au Coliseum — HOLLYWOOD PARADE —Avec LAUREL et HARDY*

*Dans un petit sketch qui les a fait se produire durant une demi-heure devant leurs admirateurs, le duo célèbre de Hollywood sortit toute la gamme de ses loufoqueries, de ses mimiques et de ses mouvements tellement personnels.*

*Ils étaient là, comme devant la caméra et l'on peut réellement écrire que l'on a retrouvé ; en quelques minutes, ce que le cinéma a immortalisé en quelques années.*

*Je sais, évidemment, qu'une bonne partie du public ne goûte pas Stan et Oliver.*

*Dame ! leur genre est tellement particulier ! On savait, par avance, ce que nos deux gaillards allaient présenter et, de ce point de vue, ils n'ont pas déçu. Ce sont deux clowns de grand talent qui ont triomphé parce qu'ils possédaient un style bien à eux.*

*Il ne fallait tout de même pas leur demander de jouer de la trompette. Au fait, c'est déjà très bien que Hardy ait chanté un des triomphes d'Al Jolson d'une voix agréable et puis qu'il ait esquissé quelques pas de danse excentriques.*

*Laurel prêt à pleurer, Hardy prêt à le battre : une explosion à gauche, leurs têtes qui se cognent, des maladresses, des mimiques, des silences; c'est cela Laurel et Hardy!*

*Les deux heures supplémentaires de spectacle furent agréables, sans plus.*

*Parmi les diverses scènes qui nous furent présentées, nous retiendrons, surtout, celle intitulée « Au nom du fisc » qui représente un ménage parvenant à convaincre le contrôleur de ne pas agir.*

*Mais il est une attraction qui égalait celle des deux grandes vedettes, une attraction incomparable.*

*L'imitateur Maxim Herman Raft ne se contente pas de singer la voix des célébrités de l'écran, mais cet homme possède de un autre don, vraiment peu banal, je vous l'assure.*

*Il contracte les traits de son visage avec tellement de bonheur, qu'il adopta successivement la physionomie de Charlie Chan, Georges Raft, Wallace Berry, Erich von Stroheim, Mathurin Popeye et Cheeta, le singe de Tarzan.*

*Son imitation de Charlie Chaplin, poussée jusque dans les moindres détails, était réellement curieuse, et j'allais dire inimitable.*

*Quand il campa Hitler, ce fut de délire dans la salle.*

*Ce qui prouve que l'on n'oublie pas les petits copains.*

*En résumé, on a été satisfait de cette soirée. On voudrait en avoir plus fréquemment de semblable, même si, comme celle-ci, elles ont des hauts et des bas.*

[ABRÉGÉ] (6<sup>th</sup> January 1948)

-----0-----

**TRANSLATION:**

At the Coliseum — HOLLYWOOD PARADE — with LAUREL et HARDY

In a sketch that lasted half-an-hour in front of their fans, the famous Hollywood duo went through the full range of their antics, their facial expressions and personal gestures. They were there, like [they are] in front of the camera, and one can really write that one found; in a few minutes, that which the cinema immortalised in a few years.

I know, obviously, that a good part of the public does not like Stan and Oliver. [WHAT?!?!?]

Lady! their kind is so special! We knew in advance that our two fellows were present and, from this point of view, they did not disappoint. These are two very talented clowns who triumphed because they had a style of their own.

There is no need to ask them to play the trumpet. In fact, it is already good that Hardy has sung one of Al Jolson hits in a pleasant voice, and then he outlined some eccentric dance steps.

Laurel ready to cry, Hardy ready to fight him: an explosion left, banging their heads, blunders, facial expressions, the silences, this is Laurel and Hardy!

*The Evening Courier* reporter interviewing the Boys backstage at the Coliseum, Verviers.

(Newspaper scan)

The extra two-hour show was fun, nothing more.

Among the various [other] scenes that were presented to us, we will remember especially one entitled "On behalf of the tax authorities" which is [about] a housewife managing to convince the Supervisor not to take action.

But it is an attraction which equalled that of the two big stars, an incomparable attraction.

The impressionist Maxim Herman Raft was not content only to mimic the voices of screen celebrities, but this man has another gift, really rather unusual, I assure you. He contracted the features of his face with so much happiness [expression??], that he successively adopted the appearance of Charlie Chan, George Raft, Wallace Berry, Erich von Stroheim, Mathurin, Popeye and Cheeta, Tarzan's chimpanzee. His imitation of Charlie Chaplin, taken down to the smallest detail, was really curious, and I would say inimitable. When he pitched his Hitler, there was delirium in the room. This proves that one does not forget little friends.

In summary, we were satisfied with the evening. We would have liked more of the same, even if, like this, they had their highs and lows.

[ABRIDGED] (*The Evening Courier* – 6th January 1948)

-----0-----

A second local newspaper, *Le Jour*, gave us:

*Nos deux compères ne connaissent virtuellement pas le français, mais le peu dont ils usent « comme ci, comme ça », ajoute encore à la drôlerie de la présentation du sketch et des chansons. Leur succès fut très grand.*

*Nous ne surprendrons personne en disant que la majorité des vedettes que nous avons connues de passage en notre ville, étaient presque toujours entourées par du remplissage de médiocre qualité, le soin de créer l'ambiance étant laissée aussi, la plupart du temps, à un infortuné pianiste.*

*Lundi, rien de tout cela ! Nous avons pû apprécier une revue « Hollywood Parade » enlevée tambour battant avec un prologue gentiment amené et deux actes où les scènes amusantes ou sentimentales ne le cédaient qu'a l'attrait crée par une troupe de 16 jolies girls à l'ensemble, au rythme et à l'entrain remarquables.*

*Des autres artistes qui se produisirent, on retiendra plus particulièrement : la danseuse acrobatique Betty Gromer, d'une souplesse et d'une adresse étonnantes ; l'imitateur, Maxim Herman-Raft vraiment extraordinaire lorsqu'il calque Charlot, Georges Raft, notre ami Donald des dessins animés etc.: le baryton Krukowski dont la voix ample et chaude, fut très appréciée.*

*La chanteuse Francine Muriel fortement enrouée (un brusque refroidissement), ne put donner la mesure de ses véritables moyens vocaux. Ce fut la seul ombre légère de cette représentation, montée avec soin et discernement, dans des décors sans prétention mais adéquats, avec, des costumes dont la fraicheur surprit agréablement et soutenue de bout en bout par un excellent orchestre (celui du Coliseum), dirigé avec beaucoup de doigté par l'auteur de l'arrangement musical de la revue, M. Emile Maetens.*

[ABRÉGÉ] (6th January 1948)

-----0-----

Backstage at the Coliseum, in Verviers.

(Newspaper scan)

**TRANSLATION:**

Our two friends know virtually no French, but the little that they use « comme ci, comme ça » ["like this, like that"] adds humour to even the presentation of the sketch and songs. They were a big success.

We will surprise no-one by saying that most of the stars we have known passing into our city, are almost always surrounded by poor quality fillers [supporting acts], the task of creating the atmosphere being left too, most of the time, to an unfortunate pianist.

Monday, none of that! We enjoyed a revue "Hollywood Parade" [enlevée tambour battant] with a gentle prologue and two acts where the amusing scenes were not inferior to that attraction created by a troupe of 16 pretty girls in all, with rhythm and in remarkable spirit.

Of the other artists who performed, we note in particular: the acrobatic dancer Betty Gromer, of an amazing flexibility and stunning skill; mimic, Maxim Herman-Raft really extraordinary when he copied Charlie Chaplin, George Raft, our friend Donald Duck from cartoons etc.; Baritone Krukowski whose ample and warm voice was much appreciated.

The singer Francine Muriel very hoarse (a sudden cold), was not able to give the measure of her true voice. It was the only slight shadow of this performance, assembled with care and discernment in unpretentious but adequate settings, with, costumes whose freshness pleasantly surprised and sustained throughout by an excellent orchestra (the Coliseum), led with great skill by the author of the musical arrangement of the magazine, Mr. Emile Maetens.

[ABRIDGED] (*The Day* – 6th January 1948)

-----0-----

### Tuesday 6th January — BRUSSELS (Bruxelles)

Tuesday morning meant making the Brussels–Verviers journey in reverse (not that they drove backwards). This time it was a more relaxing journey, for which they made the later start of 11am, and allowed, for some reason, three and a half hours to cover just seventy miles. Maybe they did it by bicycle! If they did get to the Brussels' Metropole Hotel any earlier, they would no doubt have rested up there for a short while, before making the 4:30 and 8pm shows in Brussels, itself, in a return to the Alhambra.

Backstage with one of the acts from the show at the Alhambra, Brussels.

## Wednesday 7<sup>th</sup> January — LIÈGE

Next on the itinerary was Liège, the capital of the Walloon (French-speaking) region of Belgium, situated close to the borders of both the Netherlands and Germany. The Laurels and the Hardys set off from Brussels at 10am to cover the sixty-one-mile journey east, and make an 11:30 rendezvous at the offices of *La Meuse* newspaper company. There, the official welcoming committee was made up of Mr. Ross Salmon (the tour manager for this European section), Paul Van Stalle (*ibid*), and Mr. Devaux (managing director of the Palace Theatre, Liège).

Also in attendance were MM. Fontaine, Petit, Dumont, Janssen Blonden, Foulon, and Miss Janssen, from the Royal Standard Liège Club (at whose invite the two stars would be appearing in Liège in two days' time), and M.L. Delchevalerie, President of the Northern Committee.

As the newly-formed group of visitors made its way up the stairs to the newspaper offices, the bailiff had his work cut out trying to hold back the stream of fans who wished to make contact with the screen legends.

Once in the office of the Director General of *La Meuse*, they were further welcomed by the man himself, the Knight Jean de Thier, and his top aides: Messrs. M. Tirions, Bauduin Louette Bouchat, and others.

It was Jean de Their who opened the conversation:

*« You take a drink ! » a-t-il dit à Laurel et Hardy en montrant un champagne prometteur.*

*Yes, sir !*

*Et chacun levé son verre à la ronde.*

*Voici que les conversations s'ébauchant dans un sabir ma foi fort original compromis honorable entre deux anglais souligne de gestes aussi l'expressive que possible.*

*Encore un little champagne madame ?*

*Certainly.*

*Mais leurs sketches sont en anglais seulement ? demandons à l'impresario.*

*Oui, mais un anglais — how to say it ? "très visuel"*

*Yes. I see.*

*Very, very plaisant !*

*A cigarette, sir? propose à Hardy un de nos collègues. Hardy en allume deux à la fois. Is it a gag?*

*I don't know.*

*Mais l'heure avance, et déjà arrive le moment de se séparer. C'est dommage, car je commençais à faire des progrès dans la langue de Shakespeare...*

*Laurel et Hardy redescendent l'escalier, saluent le public qui applaudit à nouveau, et tandis que les voitures démarrent ils agitent la main une dernière fois.*

[ABRÉGÉ] (Theo PIRARD. La Meuse – 7<sup>th</sup> January 1948)

-----0-----

**TRANSLATION**

"You take a drink?" he asks Laurel and Hardy, while showing [them] a promising champagne.

Yes, sir!

And everyone around raised his glass.

Still a little champagne lady?

Certainly. …

… But their sketches are in English only? asks the impresario.

Yes, but an English – how to say it? "Very visual"

Yes. I see.

Very, very nice!

A cigarette, sir? Hardy offers to one of our colleagues. Hardy lights two at the same time ... Is it a joke?

I do not know. ...

... But time moves on and already, it is time to separate. It's a shame, because I was beginning to make progress in the language of Shakespeare. ...

... Laurel and Hardy re-descend the stairs, waving to the crowd who applaud afresh, and while the cars are starting up they wave one last time.

[ABRIDGED] (*La Meuse* – 7th January 1948)

-----0-----

While Laurel and Hardy were being interviewed by the journalist from La Meuse, the caricaturist Dova drew a sketch of them, which was then published in the newspaper along with the article.

Laurel has inscribed it:
"OUR BEST WISHES A LA MEUSE SINCERELY"
Bottom line reads:
LAUREL et HARDY vus par notre caricaturiste Dova
[LAUREL et HARDY as seen by our caricaturist Dova]

It must have been a real pain for Stan and Babe to do these interviews – once you take away the free champagne. The questions were so trite, and so unrelated to their current tour, that it must have driven them to distraction (hence the reason I omitted most of the content). What made this interview even more a waste of time was that, by the time it hit the evening papers, it would have little-to-no-effect on galvanising readers into going to the show. Methinks it was more of a case of Laurel and Hardy's Belgian hosts showing-off their prized poodles.

Upon leaving the newspaper offices, the Laurel and Hardy Family booked in at the Hotel du Suéde. Shows were at 3 and 8pm.

### Thursday 8th January — GHENT (Dutch = Gent. French = Gand)

Thursday morning's journey was from Liège to Ghent, passing through Brussels. The party may possibly have stopped off in Brussels as, from leaving Liège at 9am, they had allowed three hours for what was only a ninety-three-mile road trip. Upon arriving in Ghent, they booked in at the Hotel Ville de Termonde.

Shows were at 3:30 and 8pm at the Cine Capitole. Between shows, Belgian actress Hélène Maréchal got herself a bit of free publicity, by posing for a photo with the comic legends.

Hélène Maréchal wasting the chance to get her face on camera.

Come 9th January 1948, and it was all over. Laurel and Hardy had originally left California to take up a *twelve-week* engagement; but here they were some *eleven months* later, and only now finally returning home.

The Hardys stayed on for a few days, taking a holiday with Paul van Stalle and his wife (*ibid*) before sailing from Antwerp on 15th January on board the *MV Bastogne*, bound for New York. The Laurels, meanwhile, popped over to England to spend some time visiting friends and family.

In London, Stan, *sans* Hardy, was able to move around without being pursued by the press, and it was only because he happened to attend a show business event, some two weeks later, that we have any record at all of his nineteen day break. Even then, the record comes from a source written over six years later – in this letter to his friend, Betty Healy:

August 2nd.'54

I met Mae West in London in '48 at a party after her opening in
"Diamond Lil" at the Prince of Wales Theatre, I saw the show
too, she was really sensational.

The Mae West show, *Diamond Lil*, debuted in London at the Prince of Wales Theatre, commencing 25th January 1948, before touring the UK. Stan attended the premiere – the night before. Also present at the after-show party, at Ciro's Club, were Danny Kaye – who had only just arrived in England; and Mickey Rooney – who was about to return to the States.

Just before leaving London on 28th January, to board the *Queen Mary* on its Southampton-New York crossing, Stan was waved off by a party of friends and family in the foyer of the Savoy Hotel. The family members were his sister Olga, and brother-in-law Bill Healy.

Laurel giving a farewell kiss to his sister Olga, at the Savoy Hotel, London.

(Most people aren't that passionate with their *wife*.)

Conspicuous by his absence was Stan's dad – Arthur Jefferson. "A.J" was by now in his mid-eighties, so may well have remained back at the Plough Inn, in Barkston, Lincolnshire – where he resided with his daughter Olga and son-in-law Bill. It is to be hoped that Stan had been to visit him in the days between leaving Belgium and spending time in London. It would be a great shame if he hadn't, as the great showman Arthur Jefferson passed away just one year later (15th January 1949) without the son he had imbued with so much comedy talent there to say a final farewell.

CHAPTER 12

## A FRENCH FARCE

Fourteen months after their return from Europe, Laurel and Hardy had made no films, no radio shows, nor any known personal appearances. So it was that they accepted an invite to go on a junket, by train, to and from Houston, in the company of a whole host of other Hollywood stars. At the time, Stan and Babe must have believed that this might go some way to re-establishing *themselves* as Hollywood stars. But, when the day came, Hardy had to stay behind to film his part as John Wayne's sidekick in the film *The Fighting Kentuckian*, while Laurel went on alone. When asked, on set, if his present role meant a permanent split with Laurel, Hardy was quick to give the assurance:

> "No, no. This is just temporary until we get active again. In fact, my salary goes to our joint corporation" [A reference to 'Laurel & Hardy Feature Productions'].

> Babe said he had discussed the single role with Stan, who said to go ahead. "He called me up at seven this morning to wish me luck on my first day," Hardy said.

> Hardy is going ahead with his separate career and will do a role in "Riding High" with Bing Crosby. But the boys may get back together in a picture for Glenn McCarthy Productions.

> (*Oakland Tribune* – 14th March 1949 [Abridged])

One year on, and with numerous offers of film work, stage work, and new Laurel & Hardy films to be made at the Hal Roach Studios, all coming to nought, it was an offer made back in April 1949, to go and make a film in France, which the Boys grasped with both hands. Justifying why the two Hollywood screen stars were having to leave America to get film work, Hardy referred back to the treatment meted out by Fox and MGM between 1941 and 1945:

> We'd make a deal with a studio. They'd tell you on a Friday night that they would start shooting Monday. We hadn't seen the script, and we'd say, 'Wait! We want to make it a good picture.' So they'd say, Oh! so you're getting temperamental.' Result: no picture.

And added:

> They don't seem to think a story is essential in comedy. I think it is more essential than in drama. And so many of those large studios don't want to be identified with comedy.

> (21st May 1949)

And a similar gripe in a later interview, following confirmation that Laurel and Hardy were off to Paris to make *Atoll K*.

> 'The deal sounds like the best we've had in years,' Hardy said today. 'We have a good story, and that's important.'

> 'We've had many Hollywood offers, but none have included good stories. Producers feel that all we need to do is some slapstick and that's enough.'

> (17th March 1950)

To be fair, the joint French-Italian film producers had made Laurel and Hardy a lucrative offer; but there would be a price to pay, and that price was twelve months of squabbling, frustration, despair, and life-threatening illnesses. For starters, Laurel had recently been diagnosed as diabetic. Had the two ageing comedians not had so much debt to pay off, by way of back-taxes and alimony, they might well have opted to remain in the US; which, hindsight reveals, would have been the better option – even without the film fee.

Stan and wife Ida set off for France first, sailing from New York (for Cherbourg) on the *RMS Caronia*.

They arrived in Paris on 13<sup>th</sup> April 1950 – coming in by train at St. Lazare Station, where they were greeted by a group of fans wearing masks with Oliver Hardy's likeness.

Just to show how much Laurel was missing his partner, he produced a photo of Hardy – which brought him too tears.

Using the Prince de Galles hotel as a base, Stan then spent several weeks trying to knock out a working script for the proposed film *Atoll K* with two other writers, followed soon by another two, and then yet another two replacements.

The task was almost impossible, as all had different ideas and had to try to communicate in three different languages – English, Italian, and French. Even the ones whose first language was English were incapable of getting across good comedy ideas – prompting that well-known expression: "Voici un autre désordre gentil que tu nous avez débarqués dedans."

Laurel's release, and relief, from the writing sessions was to attend public events, and to meet other acts and actors who happened to be in Paris. Letters written by him in later life reveal some of his encounters:

Oct. 17th. '57.

Dear Earl:-

Yes, George Raft has quite a background, have met him several times, last time was in Paris, France in '50. I appeared on the same radio show with him which was broadcast throughout Europe - I doubt if they understood my lousey attempt to speak French. Babe was'nt with me as I had gone ahead of him a few weeks to make preparations on the picture - story etc. so I was requested to appear alone for some publicity purpose.

[AJM: Details of the broadcast are not known, and it is considered a 'lost' tape. How come so many things are "Lost in France"?]

George Raft had come to Paris to film the appropriately titled *We Will All Go to Paris*, which is more than Laurel and Hardy had done for the Paris scenes in their film *The Flying Deuces*. Of significant interest among the cast of the former is Max Elloy, who would go on to play a principal part in *Atoll K* – that of 'Antoine – the stateless refugee.'

Following on from George Raft, another Hollywood actor whose forte was playing villainous roles was Eric Von Stroheim, of whom Laurel revealed:

Feb 22nd. '57

Dear Earl,

Yes, I know Eric Von Stroheim very well, I met him last in Paris in '50. he invited me to visit him at his home, he lives in a small village, about 30 or 40 miles from Paris but I was unable to go as I was busy making a picture. I understand he has a small beautiful estate in the country & quite a unique place, all kinds of antiques, suits of armour - old cavalry swords - muskets etc. & has a historic German horse saddle which he uses as a chair for his desk. He probably wears spurs while corresponding!

Stroheim had just returned from Hollywood after completing *Sunset Boulevard*, with Gloria Swanson and William Holden.

A third villainous character Laurel met was Russian-born Boris Morros, an independent filmmaker who had produced the Laurel & Hardy film *The Flying Deuces* for RKO, back in 1939. Morros's alleged villainy though was not on the screen, but in real life – of which Laurel makes veiled references in this letter:

July 10th.'59.

Dear Ernie [Murphy]:

I doubt if Morros was ever a 'Commie' - not to my knowledge anyway, however he was a counter-spy for the F.B.I. & his film activities was his cover up in Russia - I met him in Paris in 1950, he told me he was selling & buying films behind the Iron Curtain. I understand he is now writing a book on his experiences.

[AJM: The background to Morros's secret life was that, during the 1940s and 50s, he was a member of the KGB, but working as a double-agent for the US. The autobiography Stan refers to is *My Ten Years as a Counter-Spy* – which *was* published in 1959.]

The last time Morros had come to Laurel and Hardys notice was in April 1947, when Boris and his wife Catherine were Lucille Hardy's travelling companions aboard the *Queen Elizabeth*, on its crossing from New York to Southampton. Whether or not the three had planned to take the voyage together, or whether it was just chance, is not known. The three were acquainted, however, as Lucille had worked as script-clerk on the set of Morros's film *The Flying Deuces*, which is where she first met Babe.

Laurel with producer Boris Morros – between scenes on the set of *The Flying Deuces*. (1939)

Laurel wrote of two other talented gentlemen whom he met in Paris, but, in this instance, they were French:

```
                                              Mar. 4th. '63.

I met Maurice Chevalier a couple of times in Paris (1950) am
only just an acquaintance, but do admire his great talent.
```

Maurice Chevalier is best known for his acting role in the film *GiGi*, and as a singer with the song *Sank 'Eavens For Leetle Girls*, or *Thank Heavens For Little Girls* – as it is known in English! The second performer *may* have had a strong French accent, but one wouldn't know that from his stage work:

```
           Oct.28th. '59

Dear Mrs Hatfield:

Marcel Marceau is a French
Pantomimist - I discovered him in
Paris in 1950 & made it possible
for him to get started on his way
to success - I arranged bookings
for him in London, Eng. & he has
reached great heights ever since, &
has appeared all over the world.

He's the greatest pantomimist I've
ever seen. I feel very proud of my
protégé. Hope you will see him
work, he's a wonderful artiste.
```

Backstage with Marcel Marceau.
7th July 1947.

As for public events, on Monday 8th May Laurel was caught on camera at the *Skating Vanities* roller-skating show. In 1910 Stan had appeared several times in a Fred Karno music-hall sketch called *Skating*, in which he himself had had to demonstrate a high degree of roller-skating skills; but, forty years on, he was better off where he was – sitting in the audience.

On Tuesday 9th May he was again filmed, this time in a documentary for *Cercle Internallié* (Allied Circle), about the glory of champagne making. His fellow champagne-tasting enthusiasts included French film actor Jean Marais [far left] and actress Michèle Morgan [far right].

(Picture courtesy of Peter Mikkelsen)

On Thursday 18th May, Laurel was again among the drinks, in *A Cocktail of Stars* (the English translation of *Un Cocktail de Vedettes*). His co-drinkers Jean Marais and Michèle Morgan were again present, plus Brigitte Anber, Nicole Courcel, and Erich von Stroheim. This would have been where Stan got the invite from Stroheim to visit him at his home. Laurel's party-piece for the evening was clowning around with the musicians, pretending to play the trumpet. Again, the action was caught on film. Bravo les Francaises! who had put Laurel on film more times in just five weeks, than anyone in America had in the last five years.

Stan's next known appearance was Saturday afternoon 10th June, at the "Kermesse aux Etoiles," which translates as a "Garden Party – with Stars" – the garden in this instance being the Tuileries (Le Jardin des Tuileries) a vast park in the centre of Paris, which connects the Louvre Palace to the Arc de Triomphe on a 5-kilometer-long straight line through La Place de la Concorde and the Champs Elysees. This is where Stan would have met Maurice Chevalier, and quite possibly two other French stars in attendance, namely Simone Signoret and Yves Montand, among others. Representing Hollywood, along with Laurel, was glamorous actress-singer-dancer Rita Hayworth. But the profile of the event would have been raised most of all by the presence of no less than the French President, Vincent Auriol.

Proceeds from the fair were going to "The Veterans Fund of the French Second-Armoured Division." After inspecting some of the paratroopers and their equipment [see right], Stan went to inspect a rather more glamorous troop – or should that be 'troupe.' At the huge open-air fountain in the middle of the Tuileries a "Pageant of Beauty" had been staged, with a troupe of lovely ladies in swimwear, flitting around the perimeter of the circular fountain in synchronised moves, carrying huge beach balls. That brought a smile to Laurel's face, which the camera captures perfectly on the existing footage.

Stan was then set up at one of a series of booths, where the stars signed autographs on copies of the programme. Again we are lucky that Laurel's fund-raising antics were recorded on film.

Handing out chocolates ...                               ... signing autographs.

The original schedule for the making of *Atoll K* had been to start filming on the 15th June; but as late as the 5th June Stan had mentioned in a letter written to a relative, Nellie Bushby: "We are here to make a film in Cannes or Nice – September or October."

It would seem that the debacle over the writing of the script was the cause of the delay, and would continue to be so. However, wheels had been set in motion, and Mr. Hardy was "coming-ready-or-not." Babe and Lucille Hardy set sail for France on 10th June, on the *RMS Caronia*.

Whilst aboard, Hardy was interviewed by the ship's reporter Jack Mangan – a piece-to-camera which was filmed, and is still available to view. During it, Hardy gives a coherent account of the premise of *Atoll K*. This is nothing short of miraculous, as those who had been working on the script for the last two months weren't able to do so. Disappointingly, the earlier audio recording of Mangan's interview with Laurel, done in the latter's cabin on board the *Caronia*, seems to have been lost at sea. (At least we can't blame the French, this time.)

One has to wonder if Hardy is destroying the script which Jack Mangan worked from. Or could it be the first draft of *Atoll K*? Either way, his actions are justified.

The Hardys disembarked from the *Caronia* on 17th June, and took the train to St. Lazare Station, Paris, where Laurel was there to welcome them. When Stan had arrived, back in April, many fans had turned up wearing masks of Hardy's likeness. This time, they repeated the welcoming ceremony, but wearing masks of Laurel's likeness.

Hardy discovering Laurel is two-faced.

After a joyful reunion with Lucille and Babe, Stan joined in a game with the fans, by donning one of the Laurel masks and standing in line with the rest of the look-alikes. Babe was easily able to pick out the only Laurel in the line-up who didn't need the 'plastic surgery,' but was so thrilled when Stan removed the mask to reveal himself, that he planted a big kiss on his forehead.

LEFT: Hardy picking out the 'real' Laurel from the line-up of masked impostors.

BELOW: Babe keeping Stan at bay, while he steals a kiss from French actress Blanchette Brunoy, who has just presented him with the bouquet.

One disappointment about the Hardys' arrival was that it came a day too late to help Stan celebrate his sixtieth birthday. Maybe the Laurels and the Hardys did do some celebrating, as nothing is known of their movements for the next couple of days, although you can bet the barman in the Prince de Galles Hotel could have told you better than most.

There was, however, one immediate engagement to fulfil on the day of arrival — at a French TV studios, to do a piece for a television magazine programme called *Le Jugement de Paris*. Obviously, the idea was to announce to French viewers that Laurel and Hardy were in Paris, and also to publicise the forthcoming film; but its effect would not have been immediate as the programme was recorded, and then broadcast some two weeks later, on the afternoon of 2nd July. (Now why hadn't the BBC done just that, with the 1947 *Royal Variety Performance*?)

Laurel and his newly re-united partner Hardy were scheduled to make their first 'live' stage appearance on Thursday 22nd June, at a show titled the *Gala due Radium*, staged by the French National Opera Theatre. They were billed on advance publicity posters as "Laurel et Hardy – Les Vedettes de Atoll K" – which translates as: "the film-stars from *Atoll K*." (Good to know that, though a not a word of the script *Atoll K* had been decided upon, at least the title had.) Among those appearing at the *Gala due Radium* was legendary French singer Edith Piaf. However, at short notice, Stan and Babe had to cancel their appearance as, on that very day, they left Paris to go on a hastily arranged whistle-stop publicity tour of – ITALY.

So, with no – no regrets, of missing the opportunity to work with Edith Piaf, they set off for Italy to promote a film that did not exist — not even on paper!

CHAPTER 13

## STATION TO STATION

**Thursday 22<sup>nd</sup> June 1950 — SAN REMO** (Italian = **SANREMO**)

The first leg of the journey from Paris to Rome, for Laurel and Hardy and their wives, was the five-hundred-mile train ride from Paris to Marseilles. After a change of train, the next stop should have been at San Remo. However, the story goes that the stationmaster at Ventimiglia (a small town between Nice and San Remo, on the French-Italian border) cheekily had the train make a brief stop there, just so he could meet and greet his heroes. That makes for a good story in the local papers, but the unscheduled stop almost certainly came from a higher authority. The French Consul for Ventimiglia, M. Lecuyer, was also on his way to San Remo, to attend the same dinner as the two Hollywood comedians, so the likelihood is that it was he who arranged the stop. He might well have then travelled with them for the remaining eleven-mile journey. No matter which version is correct, the people of Ventimiglia are now able and proud to add to the town's history that: "Laurel & Hardy Stopped Here."

Upon exiting San Remo Station, the two film funny men posed for photographs with a group of locals, a few of whom were minors. Children throughout Italy would have been as well-acquainted with the films of Laurel & Hardy as Americans, Britons, and Europeans – owing to the constant showing of the films in Italian cinemas.

Within seconds of arriving, the two screen comedians are surrounded by locals.
[by kind permission of Archivio Moreschi]

The man in the white suit is Pier Busseti, manager of the Sanremo Casino, who is waiting to take the two stars and their wives to his venue.

Hardy takes the opportunity to remind himself of the times he directed a few silent films

RIGHT: Ida, Lucille, and Stan sneak off – leaving Babe to cough up the taxi fare to Pier Busseti, after being dropped off at the Sanremo Casino.

One has to wonder how many seconds it would have taken the street to fill with people, once word spread that Laurel and Hardy were there.

The cameraman who had filmed Laurel and Hardy's arrival at the station, then followed them to the Casino, where he shot additional footage. Sorry to say but, despite an exhaustive search, the whereabouts of the film remains untraced.

First directive of the day for the travelling VIPs was a quick visit to the Casino, before resting at the Royal Hotel, on Corso Imperatrice 80, in the city centre. In the evening, it was back to the Casino for an "Official Dinner" at *La Pergola Fiorita* restaurant (*The Flowered Pergola*). There is a bit of ambiguity as to whether the dinner was 'official' or whether it was a dinner *for* officials, as in attendance were a handful of French Consuls from nearby cities, plus the Chief of Police, the Commander of the Carabinieri, and the President of the Italo-French committee – all under the umbrella title of 'Regiona Authorities.'

But the evening wasn't all 'stuffed-shirts.' Some light relief was given by the very glamorous Mademoiselle ZiZi, who flirted with the two comedy stars at their table. Ida Laurel and Lucille Hardy took no umbrage though, as the lady entertainer happened to be — a marionette.

The evening at the Pergola Restaurant was going so well, with Laurel and Hardy being the thorns either side of the beautiful rose above; but then the diva below had to try and steal some of the limelight.

TOP: The lady sitting between Laurel and Hardy is Signora Pier Busseti, wife of the Casino manager

BOTTOM: Operating ZiZi is London puppeteer Frank Mumford, who can also be seen awaiting his moment – top right.

The staging of the event was coincidental to Laurel and Hardy's arrival, and was to celebrate the "Official Opening of the Season." Now we know what the adjective "official" applied to.

-----0-----

# Friday 23<sup>rd</sup> June — GENOA (Italian = GENOVA)

Just before noon, the Laurels and the Hardys boarded the train at San Remo, bound for Genoa. Lunch on board filled-in the time nicely for most of the 2hr. 40min. journey.

A slight delay was incurred when the Laurel and Hardy party tried to leave the station, owing to a traffic jam formed by the cars of all the people who turned up to see the two great comics. Once free of the station area, it was straight over to the Carlo Felice Theatre to watch a 16mm print of the 1933 Laurel & Hardy film operetta *Fra Diavolo*, dubbed into Italian.

It was the first time this magnificent theatre had been used to screen a film, but the management weren't going to make any financial gain from it, as the two stars stipulated that the box-

Ida Laurel (with back to camera), Stan, Babe, and Lucille Hardy about to be seated in the Carlo Felice Theatre, GENOA

office takings should go to a charity of their choice – the 'War Orphans Benefit' – more specifically, the 'Institute of Blind and War-wounded Kids of Padre Umile' (a Capuchin).

A squad of policemen ringing the Hollywood legends as they exit the Carlo Felice Theatre, into Via Roma. (Hardy is partly hidden by the policeman in dark uniform, centre.)

After the screening, the Boys hosted a Press Conference and small cocktail party at the offices of the "Associazione Ligure dei Giornalisti" (Liguria Association of Journalists), in the Piazza De Ferrari, at which reporters were encouraged to ask questions about the *Atoll K* project.

[AJM: Liguria is a coastal region of north-western Italy, of which Genoa is the capital.]

Organiser of this Genoa leg of the tour was businesswoman Ebe Roisecco, who was employed by the film company Universalia as a counsellor. Ms. Roisecco, who along with Enzo De Bernart had welcomed the VIPs at the station, next acted as hostess at a big party at the "Associazione Italo-Americana" in a restaurant atop its office building.

Before arriving in Genoa, Stan and Babe had been told that they had the freedom to do and see what they wished to, but, following all the events laid on for them, it would seem that any free time had been taken up, and so they most likely just retired to their hotel, the Miramare.

### HOTEL MIRAMARE – Portofino

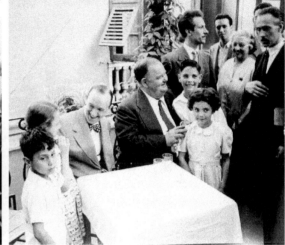

It would be nice for Laurel and Hardy to
enjoy a quiet drink with their wives …

… the problem was –
they were Laurel & Hardy.

## Saturday 24<sup>th</sup> June — MILAN (Italian = MILANO)

A bright and early start on Saturday morning had them leaving Genoa at 9:35am, for a noon arrival in Milan — where, again, they were mobbed by hundreds of fans at the rail station.

Even after escaping the crush on the station platform, the Laurels and the Hardys
found themselves surrounded by fans, police, and cameramen, as they tried to exit .

The schedule was on similar lines to the previous two: private lunch – rest – Press Conference – and private dinner. The first two items on the agenda were conducted at the Hotel dei Cavalieri; then, early afternoon, it was over to the Italian radio station EIRA for 'on air' interview.

The presenter of the radio show "*Voci dal Mondo*" (*Voices of the World*) was Vittorio Veltroni (father of Walter Veltroni, an Italian politician in Milan). One of the guests was pressman Emilio Pozzi. Earlier, Emilio had greeted the Boys at the train station, and managed to get a few words out of them, which he then very loosely translated LIVE on the Radio Program *Il Gazzettino Padano*, at 12.40pm. But then, at the afternoon radio show with L&H, Emilio was somewhat conspicuous by his lack of dialogue – the reason behind which will be revealed a little later.

Another guest was Carlo Dapporto, a well-known Italian singer and actor. Dapporto began his show business career in 1935 doing an impression of Stan Laurel, along with partner Carlo Campanini, as Oliver Hardy. Here, in the absence of his partner, Dapporto was also able to do a passable vocal impression of Ollie, which came in very useful. Whenever either Stan or Babe said something in English, Carlo was able, not only to repeat it to listeners in Italian, but to say it in the respective voice. Funny AND clever.

Carlo Dapporto doing a fine facial impression of Laurel.

Between Babe and Stan, holding the mic,
is Emilio Pozzi – a man of few words.

As for Emilio Pozzi, he didn't speak a word of English throughout the whole programme. When the interview ended, Stan asked Emilio "Why you didn't talk at all? Did you forget your English?" to which Dapporto had to explain that Emilio couldn't speak *any* English, adding: "Those four questions he asked you are the only words of English he knows. He was taught them just before he met you." This broke up Stan and Babe, who had totally believed that Emilio was fluent in English. Pozzi went on to dine out at many free dinners to come, regaling his table companions with the story of how he made Stanlio and Ollio laugh.

From the photos it is quite obvious that it wasn't only the listeners who were having a good laugh, but sorry to report that, despite several enquiries by L&H fans, the recording has never been traced – if indeed one exists. Still, having the photos and story behind them does, I trust you will agree, come a close second.

All that was now left to do from the pre-arranged schedule was for Laurel and Hardy to attend a private dinner. That was, until someone, in their wisdom, managed to lever in another film show for them to attend. And guess what! — it was the same film they had viewed in Genoa, *Fra Diavolo*. It gets worse: There were TWO showings – one at 3pm and 5.30pm, although it is doubtful that Laurel and Hardy stayed on to watch the full film even once, as they were off to get ready for that private dinner.

Ariston Cinema – MILAN

Look! That's me.                                    And who do you think you are?

After walking on stage and addressing the audience, at the Ariston Cinema, Laurel and Hardy did see some of the film (maybe only the trailer) as Laurel was to mention the event in a letter some thirteen years later.

```
                                                    APRIL 20th.'63

Dear Elmer:

The L&H film version of 'Fra Diavalo' is still shown every year
in Italy, it was showing in Milan when Hardy and I were there
in 1950, the English was 'dubbed' in Italian language, I got a
big kick out of L&H speaking Italian just like the natives!
```

[AJM: This 1950 screening was the thirteenth time *Fra Diavolo* (aka: *The Devil's Brother*) had been released in Milan. The fact that *Fra Diavolo* is based in Italy has more than a little to do with its popularity. The equivalent to cinemagoers in England would be an Italian film about *Robin Hood*. In the former, the eponymous villain is named as "The Marquis de San Marco," – a name which may owe its origins to San Marco in Lamis, in the Apulia region of southeast Italy. San Marco ("St. Marks") is also the name of the main piazza in Venice.]

For their one-day and one-night-stay in Milan, the Laurel and Hardy party had been booked into the Hotel Dei Cavalieri. The 'night' though, turned out to be the shortest night of the year, as they booked out just after midnight, and at 1am boarded the train for Rome. They wouldn't be denied sleep though, as sleeping-berths had been booked for the 9hr. 45min. train ride. The spectacle of the scene awaiting them in Rome was, however, something they could never have dreamt of.

CHAPTER 14

## THROWN TO THE LIONS

### Sunday 25<sup>th</sup> June — ROME (Italian = ROMA)

The train duly pulled in at 10:45am at Rome's Stazione Termini. As the Laurel and Hardy party alighted, the first thing to hit them was the sound of the 40-piece Giuseppe Verdi Marching Band blasting out the now-customary *Cuckoo Song*.

The visiting party's next sense to be hit was by the sight of the hundreds of people crammed onto the platform, many of whom were holding balloons bearing their names and likenesses. Others were holding up placards, with messages painted on them such as: "STANLIO ER CHIODO," meaning: "Stanlio the spike" – which is a friendly Roman slang nickname. [I suppose it refers to Laurel's spikey hair]. Another placard read:

"AD OLLIO ER CICCIONE E STANLIO ER SECCARDINO, CHE A FORZA DE FACCE RIDE CIANNO FATTO SCORDA' LI GUAI NOSTRI" – meaning: "TO OLLIO THE FAT ONE AND STAN THE SKINNY ONE, WHO MADE US FORGET OUR TROUBLES BY MAKING US LAUGH."

But then, things began to get out of control. Some over-enthusiastic fans picked up Laurel and began to carry him, shoulder-high, through the station — which is not a good thing to do to a sixty-year-old unfit man. At least they didn't give him "the bumps," to mark his birthday nine days earlier.

Laurel being carried aloft. Wisely, Hardy was left with his feet on 'good old terra cotta.'
(In case you are still wondering – Stan and Babe are holding bouquets of flowers,
wrapped in cellophane, and mounted on sticks.)

The policemen on hand to protect the two stars were unable to prevent the unwanted physical contact, so concentrated their energies on forcing a way through the crowd, to the exit. Whereas the Laurels and the Hardys would have liked to walk along as a foursome, they were now reduced to being led, in single file, with the police escort at the head – which rather resembled the ancient ceremony of the Christians being led into the Colosseum amphitheatre. Thankfully, the foreigners weren't thrown to the lions; although, while running the gauntlet through the baying crowd, the two screen stars were pawed, clawed and mauled from all sides.

[AJM: The action was caught on movie-camera by two different newsreel companies, but the one known extant piece of footage is so short that it is a case of: "blink, and you'll miss it."]

Thankfully, both Stan and Babe did make it through the crowd unharmed, but weren't in the clear just yet, as they were shepherded to the "Piazza del Cinquecento," where they had been invited to inaugurate the new entrance hall of the station. There was a slight delay while Lucille Hardy and Ida Laurel found their way to the Boys' new location, as the two ladies had got split off in the melee.

Stan and Babe had now been joined by Italian actor Walter Chiari [See right, in the white suit!] who had been sent by Universalia to welcome the stars of their latest film, to Rome. Chiari had been chosen as he was one of the actors on the short list for a part in *Atoll K*, but was later passed over for, it is thought, Adriano Rimoldi.

Chiari did an impression of Stan in some of his own pictures, which he had practised by watching the Laurel & Hardy films from the thirties; and then, between 1946 and 1950, almost ALL the Laurel & Hardy films had been released throughout Italy, many for the first time. So, when Chiari met the two comedy actors 'live,' he was troubled by seeing Stan so skinny and Ollie so huge — about which he commented: "Peccato averli visti dal vivo." (Translation: "It was a bit sad seeing them for real.") He thought they looked too old for films, which sums up what most people would come to say upon seeing the finished film *Atoll K*.

Upon leaving the Termini Station, the two stars had to dash outside and jump into the waiting red leather-upholstered Cabriolet car, whilst their wives took a second car behind them. With the assistance of a police escort, the motorcade then slowly made its way through the vast throng, to the Grand Hotel. Because the Grand (now the St. Regis.) is so close to the station, many fans simply followed the car, and joined the already significant number awaiting the arrival of the comedy couple.

A grand gesture – from the Grand Hotel.

Here, what had now become customary practice was put in force. With the ever-growing crowd outside clamouring to see them, Stan and Babe ascended to the roof of the Grand, and conducted their salutations from there. The fans cheered and shouted for what seemed like an eternity, and just wouldn't let the two screen stars retire inside. On-lookers from afar may well have thought it was the Pope up there, addressing his congregation.

Lunch was a private affair in the hotel, but then at 6pm Laurel and Hardy were Guests of Honour at a Garden Party, organised by "The Comune of Rome" to raise money for "The Children of Rome" — the children in question being orphans. Again Stan and Babe were mobbed as soon as they stepped outside the hotel, but they were loving every minute of it. Hey! When you've been treated as has-beens in your own country for five years, this makes for a very pleasant change. However, the scenes of joy almost turned to one of tragedy:

The show took place at the Villa Aldobrandini, on a stage erected in the open circular courtyard. (See right!). The audience did contain many adults but, because all the children had been admitted free, the number of admissions soon grew to around three thousand. It was hosted by Alberto Sordi, who introduced a puppet act and then a competition to find the best Laurel & Hardy impersonators, before bringing the screen legends themselves on stage.

Alberto Sordi, himself, was one half of a Laurel & Hardy tribute act. He did the voice of Ollie, while his partner, Mauro Zambuto, played Stan. Both were on hand that day to translate what the real Laurel and Hardy were saying on stage, by repeating it back to the audience – except in Italian. The children and adults alike, therefore, had the novelty of being able to compare the real voices with the ones they were used to hearing when watching the films of Laurel & Hardy, as it was actually Sordi and Zambuto who did the dubbing for the films released in Italy.

Things were going really well – too well, in fact, as the children got over-excited and swarmed the stage, which resulted in Stan and Babe having to be spirited away by a squad of police bodyguards. In a panic, Alberto Sordi jumped into his car but, in his haste to escape, knocked down an old lady. Thankfully, she wasn't injured, and Stan and Babe were able to continue their public appearances, without a dark cloud being cast over the visit to Rome. It had been a close call.

LEFT: Zambuto and Sordi dubbing the Laurel & Hardy film *A Chump at Oxford* (released in Italy in 1946).

The evening found the Laurels and the Hardys having dinner at the Open Gate Club, in Via Veneto. Their hostess was Marchioness Altoviti (married to marquise Antonio Niccolai Lazzerini Altoviti Avila). Throughout the dinner most of Marchioness Altoviti's conversation was with Lucille Hardy. Sitting next to Babe Hardy was Alberto Sordi, who talked to him at length about their movies and why, apart from *Atoll K*, he and his partner had had no other film offers for several years. Sordi was very touched by observing this fallen star, and spoke about him regularly with respect and sentiment for the rest of his life.

It must be assumed that Mauro Zambuto accompanied Sordi at the dinner. Zambuto recalled in an interview with Benedetto Gemma in 2000 (recorded by Avv. Antonio Costa Barbé), that he was stunned when he saw Stan and Oliver in person. "Oliver was a giant," he said, "a mountain," and: "Stan was also very tall, a big person, but much too skinny, and exhausted, as if someone kept him in formaldehyde!"

[AJM: If Zambuto thought Laurel was skinny, and looked as if he was preserved in formaldehyde, what would he think in a few months' time, when Laurel became really ill? Read on!]

## Monday 26th June — ROME (Day 2)

After lunch, Laurel and Hardy were interviewed on two radio shows (the recordings of which appear to be 'lost') and then at 6pm did a Press Conference – most likely in the hotel. In the evening, the Boys left the safety of the Grand Hotel to attend a party, held in their honour, at the Casina Valadier, a restaurant situated on the Monte Pincio – a hilltop with an impressive view over Rome (although NOT one of "the seven hills of Rome").

Their host was Italian film producer Salvo d'Angelo, the man who had originated the idea of using these two Hollywood comedians in a film. D'Angelo had originally intended producing the film through his own film company – "Universalia Produzione," but was unable to raise all the finance himself. He had then approached the French production company "Franco-London-Films S.A." – with whom he had successfully collaborated on the film *La Beauté du Diable* (1950) – and they agreed to co-produce *Atoll K*. As this was now a French-Italian co-production, D'Angelo wanted to promote the film in Italy, and that is how the two stars came to be doing these pre-production publicity appearances.

Salvo d'Angelo finally gets to meet the stars of his latest film.

[AJM: On Laurel and Hardy's schedule was a note saying: "… between the 25-26-27 the meeting with the President will be fixed by his private Secretary." As this was written on a letter issued by Enzo De Bernart, the Press Officer for Universalia Produzione, it is thought that it refers NOT to the President of the Republic of Italy, but to the President of the company — that President being Salvo d'Angelo.]

Laurel could be saying to the young lady: "If we hold hands across Hardy's chest, we can stop him eating AND smoking."

Among the guests of mainly film and publicity people was the Belgian Dominican – Felix Andrew Morlion. Father Morlion was associated with the publishing house "Katholieken Filmliga" via his film press agency DOCIP (Documentation Cinématique Presse). He also acted as advisor/censor for the Belgian cinema industry, which involved searching through films to track down any scenes which might offend the Catholic Church.

It is also alleged that the American Secret Service OSS (Office of Strategic Services), the precursor of the CIA, had financed Father Morlion's organisation "Pro Deo" in Lissabon and the USA (in 1943). If so, then

Morlion can be considered to have been the founder of the Secret Service of the European Catholics; working for the CIA under the cover of the International Catholic University of the Vatican "Pro Deo." His real-life story seems to have more political intrigue than fictional story of *Atoll K*. But was he funny??

Hardy pointing out that Father Morlion has the same receding hairline as him and his partner.
[With sincere thanks to Michael Ehret for the photo, and the tremendous background story.]

Other known guests at the party were Walter Chiari (*ibid*), and John Pasetti, who did an audio interview for Swiss Radio (yet another 'lost' recording).

On the itinerary given to Laurel and Hardy by the Universalia Produzione Press Office (*ibid*), the entry for the day after the party (Tuesday 27th June) proposed a full day of free time in Rome; worded as, "whatever you want to do." For the Wednesday there was a rather more memorable and exciting event planned – namely: "Visit to the Pope." Appended was the clause: "Should you want to make your visit shorter, we would try to have the Pope's visit on Monday the 26th instead of the 28th."

It is a distinct possibility that Father Morlion had attended the party at the Casina Valadier, specifically to arrange for Laurel and Hardy's audience with the Pope. How hilarious to have been privy to Pope Pio XII saying: "If they won't come to see me on Wednesday, tell them I'll change my schedule so that they can come on Monday."

As it happened, the Laurel and Hardy party left on Tuesday the 27th, and so did not get to see the Pope at all. You have to laugh when you think of two men from such humble backgrounds telling their friends and relatives: "When we were in Rome, the Pope wanted to meet us, but we had more important things to do, and left without seeing him."

So it was that the Laurels and the Hardys departed from Rome a day earlier than expected, to attend to more important matters back in Paris. This time, they weren't about to break their journey, as they had done on the way to Rome, but were taking the much faster, and more comfortable option of a Pullman sleeping-car on the luxurious 'Compagnie Internationale Des Wagons Lits et Des Grands Express Europeens.' (International Company of Sleeping Cars and the Grand European Expresses).

Ollie ordering Stanley onto the train,
before it moves off.
Rome rail station – 27th June
(Superimposed image – by Benedetto Gemma)

The Hollywood stars' departure had not been made public so, in direct contrast to the scene upon their arrival in Rome, the platform was pretty much deserted. Thankfully, though, there was a photographer on hand to capture the comedians' last gestures and waves of "Farewell" to the 'Eternal City'— a city which would remain eternally etched in their minds and hearts.

On Rome Station, waving 'Goodbye' from "Des Wagons Lits et Des Grands Express Europeens."

Some ten hours later, the Grand European Express made a short stop in Turin (10:30pm), where masses of people, having been notified of Laurel and Hardy's presence on board, had turned out to see them. This caught the Boys totally unawares. So much so, that Hardy, in responding to the calls of the crowd to show themselves, appeared at the window minus his trousers. (Please, let us all take it for granted he was wearing his undershorts.) The reason for his state of semi-undress was because it was a particularly hot and sticky June night, and being inside the sleeping car was like being in a sauna.

With no one fainting at the sight of Hardy's appearances, and pleased to have seen the faces they had only previously seen upon on the big screen, the Italian fans waved "arrivederci" as the train pulled out to complete the remaining estimated ten-hour journey from Turin to Paris.

Meanwhile, as the express sped through the night, it would be funny to imagine the Pope being too excited to sleep, owing to the thought of meeting his comedy idols the following day.

# CHAPTER 15

## NOT ATOLL WELL

Once Stan and Babe were back in Paris, getting the shooting-script for *Atoll K* finished would have been the first priority. However, on the Saturday of 1st July the comedy couple attended yet another festive event, billed as "La Grande Nuit de Paris." The group of mask-wearing fans who had met both Laurel AND Hardy when they first arrived in Paris, had gone there with the primary reason of coercing the two Hollywood stars into attending this event, hence the banners you will see in the earlier photograph.

"La Grande Nuit de Paris" translates as: "Paris's Big Night." And a 'Big Night' it was too, with around 250,000 revellers in attendance, plus a sprinkling of French and American stars of stage and screen. It was an open-air event, held at the Palais de Chaillot on the banks of the Seine, close to the Eiffel Tower. A show made up of live performers, plus excerpts from other shows, had been devised. The first-half was presented on a stage specially-built on the steps of the Palais de Chaillot. The second half incorporated a two-ton lighting rig on a canopy, suspended high above the Seine. However, when a safety check revealed that the rig didn't have enough supports to take the vast weight, the whole second-half of the show had to be cancelled. As it was 2:15am by then, perhaps the crowd weren't too disappointed.

**"The Big Night of Paris and Stan LAUREL wish the welcome to Oliver HARDY"**
[Note the mis-spelling of Hardy's first name, due to a mix-up with that well-known Shakespearean actor and film star — Laurel Olivier.]

Thankfully, the first half went off well, with Patachou, Larry Adler, Bourvil, Eddie Cantor, Edith Piaf, Stan Laurel and Oliver Hardy, and Charles Trénet, all turning in performances.

Eddie Cantor and Stan Laurel seem to be experiencing the effects of a romantic starlit Parisian night.

Cantor sang choruses of *Margie*, and *If You Knew Suzie*; Edith Piaf fitted in the usual trills and much "r"-rolling into her numbers; and Charles Trenet finished with his legendary classic *La Mer*. Good to see that Stan and Babe *DID* get to appear with Piaf, after all.

Stan and Ollie's performance was a little less vocal. Because of the number of people present, coupled with the viewing restrictions, and the limitations of the sound-system, they realised that performing a sketch wouldn't work, so they just did an improvised comic entrance. (Is anyone experiencing déjà vu?) From the extant audio recording we can glean most of their routine, as follows:

The compere introduces Laurel and Hardy, and we hear their signature tune *The Cuckoo Song*. The Boys walk out, but the tempo is too fast for them and they are unable to make a dignified entrance. The compere isn't happy and, while telling them to try again, ushers them off. The music repeats, but this time the tempo is too slow, and their entrance again fails to impress. One can only surmise that Stan mimed some exasperated open-arm appeals, and Hardy gave his "looks-to-camera" to the audience. Hardy then gives a tie-twiddle, so it must be presumed Laurel did 'a head-scratch' followed by 'a cry' – and it was all over.

One has to contemplate the possibility that this expanded walk-on was devised following lessons learned from their experience at the Antwerp Sportpaleis. As Laurel might well have said: "Necessity is the mother of infection!"

Profits from "La Grande Nuit" went to the "Orphanages of Paris." At the climax there was a huge firework display, which was filmed. In one particular shot, a sky-burst illuminates the spectators below, and we get a glimpse of two very familiar faces – Stan and Babe.

"La Grande Nuit de Paris" was staged annually to mark the end of the season. How puzzling that Laurel and Hardy had been present at the OPENING of the season in San Remo and yet, just nine days later, the CLOSING of the season in Paris. Short season! I've made a loaf of bread last longer than that. (Not French bread, though!)

Continuing work on the script prompted a script meeting for which, on 16th July, the two comedy stars had to travel to the Cote d'Azur. This was almost certainly a locations reconnaissance, to see what aspects of the topography they could, or could not, incorporate into the film. Once satisfied, the stars, writers, and production crew returned to Paris.

Three more weeks of late nights, wet towels, and a plentiful supply of coffee, finally led to a script that was thought to be workable; and so, on 5th August, everyone set off for Marseilles to start filming.

ABOVE: It all started off so well, when Laurel and Hardy went to board the train for Marseilles ...

... but a problem arose when actors Max Elloy and Suzy Delair tried to get Hardy into the sleeping car.

The overnight sleeper from the Gare du Lyon in Paris got them to Gare St. Charles in Marseilles, on the morning of 6th August, from where they retired to the Hotel Bristol.

Film still of the scene with the boys arriving at
Marseilles Harbour. (Filmed 7<sup>th</sup> August 1950)

The next seven or eight days were spent in Marseilles Harbour, shooting the outdoor scenes where, in the film, Stan and Ollie meet 'Antoine the stateless man' (played by the aforementioned Max Elloy) before sailing off on their newly-acquired boat.

Away from filming, they did find time to make a public appearance, which was judging the semi-finals of an accordion-playing competition, at the theatre Silvain in Marseilles itself (Thursday 10<sup>th</sup> August).

From Marseilles, cast and crew moved approximately one hundred and thirty miles eastward along the coast, to Raphael on the Cote d'Azur, where shooting commenced on 16<sup>th</sup> August. The island identified in the film as "Atoll K" wasn't technically an island at all, but a peninsular called Cap Roux, near Cannes, joined to the mainland by an isthmus. This is where a mock-up of their boat, the *Momus*, had been brought from Paris and suitably distressed to look like a beached wreck. Later "the wreck" of the *Momus* would be returned to the studios in Paris, where the rest of the scenes were to be filmed.

Although, when not working, Stan and Babe and their wives were able to relax in comfort at the Hotel Excelsior, in St. Raphael, the hardships of the daytime shooting, especially the heat, began to cause the Boys severe health problems. During the 1947-48 tour of the Continent, Hardy had shed 75 pounds, and wasn't happy with the experience: "I tasted my first whale meat, and my first horse meat," he said sourly.

The whale meat must have finally taken effect as he had put back on all the lost weight, and more, making him around

Enjoying a musical break in the Hotel Excelsior, with an
accordionist they possibly met at the show in Marseilles.

330 pounds (23st 8lbs). The excess weight he was carrying, combined with the daily dose of intense heat he was being subjected to, caused him to develop heart fibrillation – a condition described as: "Rapid chaotic beating of the heart muscles in which the affected part of the heart may stop pumping blood."

As for Laurel, he was losing weight faster than Hardy was gaining it. His diabetes caused enough limitations; but when he was attacked by a further medical problem (which I don't wish to describe) the effects rendered him extremely weak and unable to film for more than thirty minutes at a time.

# HARDY HOLIDAY SNAPS

While the director and crew run through the next scene, aboard the *Momus*, moored in Marseilles Harbour, Hardy takes a moment out to pose for his wife Lucille.

The seaward end of Cap Roux, with the wreck of the *Momus* in the background

Lucille and Babe setting up for a picnic on the beach at Cap Roux.

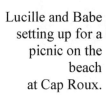

Film still of the scene in which the Boys show Chérie Lamour (Suzy Delair) the makeover they have done on her hut.

After Hardy has been caught several times flirting outrageously with co-star Suzy Delair between filming, Lucille Hardy sticks around to keep a closer eye on him.

(From the Paul E. Gierucki Collection)

Without their two stand-ins, Julien Maffre and Victor Decottignies,
Stan and Babe would have been in even more of a nice mess.

Stan struggled gainfully on and, God bless him, managed to shoot all the on-location scenes, plus those done at the Victorine Studios, in Nice, over the immediate weeks. But, by then, he was in a pretty serious condition; and so, the minute the film company was dismissed, he was sent off to Paris to rest and recuperate. But rest and recuperation were not going to be enough. Something was very wrong. On 10th October he was admitted to the American Hospital, where, following nearly three weeks of deliberation, he had an operation to remove an internal abscess. (Don't ask!)

On 21st November, after six weeks in hospital, Laurel was deemed fit enough to be discharged. To illustrate how well he was feeling, just two nights later he was photographed dancing in a Paris nightclub. And who was his dance partner, the one who had given him the strength and will to have a night out on the town? Why it was none other than – Oliver Norvell Hardy. Some people think he thought more of Hardy than he did of his wife. Well we won't go into that!!

But it was all a brave act. Stan wasn't well at all, and spent the next six weeks trying to recover, and to put back some of the weight he had lost during his illness. In this he was aided by the tender loving care of his wife, Ida, who looked after his every need in their suite at the Hotel D'lena, on the Avenue D'lena, in Paris.

Hardy, though, wasn't confined to bed, and attended the New Year's Eve celebrations at the restaurant La Tour d'Argent (The Money Tower. Or is it "The Silver Tower"?) with new screen-partner Suzy Delair, the French film actress co-starring in *Atoll K*. It was a double celebration as the 31st December also happened to be Suzy's birthday, which gave Hardy, who was obviously smitten by her, even more licence to plant kisses on her lovely countenance.

The start of the New Year didn't bring forth the hoped-for change in fortune, as Laurel again had to be admitted to hospital. As he explained in a letter to a close friend written some six years later:

"LUCiiiiiiiiiiiiiiiiiiiiiLLE – he's at it, again."

July 14th. '56.

Dear Betty Healy:-

I got over my operation Ok, but suffered a great deal more
later due to the conglomeration of pills & shots they gave
me to help the original trouble. I ended up having chronic
dysentery for nine straight months, then I had to take more
medicines to cure that. I think probably my whole system
was poisoned & became one of the reasons for my stroke.

Hardy went to bring him 'home' on 9th January, and on the 17th the two were able to recommence filming at the Franco-London Films Studio in Billancourt – a suburb of Paris.

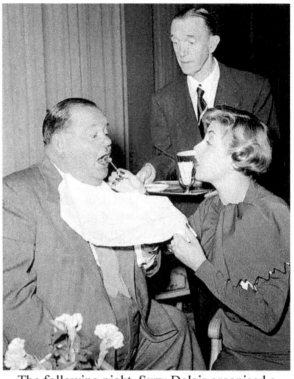

Hardy escorting his partner from the
hospital to his suite at the Hotel D'Iena.
9th January 1951

The following night, Suzy Delair organised a
party to welcome Laurel back, but it's Hardy
getting all the bedside nursing.

On set the following day, shooting was again interrupted. With months of delays already accrued, the company didn't need further ones, but everyone was quite happy over this halt in filming, as it was for the present-ation of a huge cake and a magnum of champagne to celebrate Hardy's 59th Birthday. Another excuse for Babe to have more kisses off Suzy!

It looks like Suzy Delair is trying
to make Hardy *sneeze* out, rather
than *blow* out, his candles.

Another interruption, but another welcome one, was a visit to the set by Hollywood cowboy and general tough guy John Wayne. Wayne was over in France promoting his recently released film *Sands of Iwo Jima*, and had popped round to see his buddy, and fellow-member of the Masquers Club, Oliver Hardy.

Michel Dalmatoff, Herb Yates (President of Republic Pictures), Adriano Rimoldi, Hardy, John Wayne, Suzy, Laurel, Max Elloy.

In 1949 Hardy had spent a happy time with Wayne, during filming of *The Fighting* Kentuckian, so it was a joyful reunion (although Wayne's face never came close to portraying joy).

Laurel, Hardy, Suzy, Max Elloy, Simon van Collem (journalist) Adriano Rimoldi, Michel Dalmatoff

At the end of March 1951, Stan Laurel and Oliver Hardy finally heard, what was for them at the time, the most glorious four-letter word in the English language – "It's a WRAP."

## CHAPTER 16

### NO RETURN

The Boys had gone to France expecting to spend just twelve weeks there. This had turned into twelve MONTHS – twelve months of sheer torture. Having waited six years to regain their credibility as filmmakers, Laurel and Hardy had been dealt the cruellest of blows in the making of this one. And so, in February 1951, a deal for them to go to Australia to make another film had been dismissed without hesitation.

By some form of malicious irony, *Atoll K* was to receive just about the biggest promotion, and exploitation, of all of the one-hundred-plus Laurel & Hardy films. The film was eventually released in three dubbed language versions, and in varying lengths, depending on what the various releasing companies deemed worth, or not worth, leaving in. Different cuts of the film were released under different titles. The version released in the UK, in February 1952, was known as *Robinson Crusoeland*, while other countries received the film as *Utopia*.

| DANISH poster | SPANISH poster | FRENCH poster |

No matter which version you watch, you can't help but notice Laurel metamorphosing from one hundred and sixty-five pounds to one hundred and fourteen — that is, if you can bear to watch it through. Actually, once you accustom yourself to Laurel's gaunt look, it is not a bad film. It is certainly better than nearly all of the Fox and MGM films they made. At least in *Atoll K*, the two stars did have control over the script and characters they were playing. So, if you haven't yet seen it, my advice would be to give it a try. It will be your way of thanking the Boys for all the sacrifice they made to see it through so as not to let down their fans.

Stan and Babe may well have had it in their minds that they *would* consider accepting future film offers but, at that moment in time, just wanted to retreat to their den and lick their wounds. Little did they know but, on the filmmaking front, Laurel & Hardy had made the final cut. From now on, the stage would be the only medium in which they were to work.

Stan Laurel wasn't going to extend his stay in France by one day more than was necessary. He and Ida left France on 17th April 1951, aboard the *RMS Queen Elizabeth*, and sailed for home – by-passing England this time around.

| From the boat train … | … to the boat |

The Hardys, meanwhile, were happy to stay on for a short holiday with, it is thought, Paul Van Stalle and his wife, from the Brussels Alhambra (*ibid*); before departing from Belgium on 23$^{rd}$ April, aboard the *MS Washington*.

Back in California, none of the numerous deals Laurel and Hardy had been offered, before or since leaving a year ago, had come to fruition. But, just when it looked as though they might never work again, fate *seemed* to relent. Without doing anything whatsoever, they were suddenly in demand by everyone. The cause of the upsurge was that, during the mushrooming-spread of television throughout America, selections from the fifty-two Laurel & Hardy shorts which Hal Roach had sold to a TV network were now being given regular screenings. Consequently, TV viewers were clamouring for more — old ones, AND new ones. The Boys' old pal, Hollywood columnist Erskine Johnson, interviewed them on the subject:

> For the first time in five years Stan Laurel and Oliver Hardy will be on your neighbourhood theatre screens this winter in a feature comedy, "Atoll K." And they're being deluged with TV offers.
>
> "A whole new generation of kids have discovered us," Hardy beamed.
>
> There are no big casts and no big flossy production numbers in the blueprints for new Laurel and Hardy comedies, whether they are for TV or movie theatres.
>
> "It will be the same situation comedy," Hardy made it clear, "with one set and no more than three other actors in the cast. We have to be together. Split us up and put us with other people and we're gone. Everything that happens to us happens in a little corner."
>
> "Laurel, as usual, will be supervising and helping us write the scripts."
>
> "We've been accused of being temperamental because we want to supervise our own stuff," Hardy let it fly. "Well, that's not true. We know just what's right for us."
>
> "We refused to do a picture for a certain producer at Fox. He called us to his office and said:"
>
> "Sit down, boys, and tell me what you don't like in the script."
>
> "We asked him, 'Have you read it?'"
>
> "He replied:" "'Well, no, I've been a busy man lately.'"
>
> "That's when we quit. How can you do a movie when the producer hasn't even read the script?"
>
> (16$^{th}$ November 1951)

107

But it wasn't only American television programme-makers who wanted Laurel & Hardy. According to a letter written by Stan to Betty Healy, interest was coming in from the Continent:

```
                                          June 20th.'51.

Dear Betty:-

I was in the hospital only a couple of days - just an
examination for something due to my operation in Paris last
year - nothing serious & all is OK. I understand Louella
Parsons true to form, gave me the last Rites over the air.

Expect to leave for Italy - France & Spain for a years run in a
Revue about Sept - if the War business does'nt upset our plans.
```

[AJM: By "war business" I believe Laurel is referring to the 'General Strike of 1951' – which started in Barcelona, and then spread to many other parts of Spain. An estimated 300,000 workers were eventually involved, which caused the authorities to mobilise police and Civil Guard units to quell the street riots. Thousands of strikers were imprisoned until the strike was eventually broken.]

From the day he received his very first fan letter, Stan Laurel went out of his way to reply to every single one. During the height of his film career this would not have been physically possible, but certainly, from 1946 onwards, he did his utmost to stick to this principle. He once told a reporter: *"If I didn't reply, people would think I was high and mighty."*

I don't believe anyone would have thought that at all, but the compelling drive to write back stayed with Stan till the very end.

The peak of his letter writing was in 1957 when he told a friend: "I've written over one thousand letters this year:" If you don't think that sounds like many, try writing three letters per day, every day, for a whole year.

Laurel even continued replying to fans when a stroke left him partially paralysed, and without vision in one eye. God bless him!

In Laurel's next letter to Betty Healy (widow of Ted Healy, who created 'The Three Stooges'), there was no mention of the European bookings, but there *had been* a better development these six months farther on:

```
                                          December 6th. '51

My Dear Betty:-

Glad to tell you, I never felt better, I now weigh 149 lbs
and look like my old self again & expect to leave for
England in February for personal appearances also
Television shorts over there. Needless to tell you I can't
wait to get back in harness again. To be very frank I never
thought I would, last year at this time I weighed only 110
lbs. I shall know definitely next week re the trip so of
course will let you know.

Well Betty, will close now. Am busy digging up a new act to
take over, know you understand.
```

Eleven days later, the details were confirmed:

December 17th. '51

Dear Betty:

We are leaving for England end of January, due in London
Feb. 3rd. so as you can imagine I am up to my neck in
preparation, a million & one things to do.

Yes, Babe is going too. Our name L&H is magic over there,
it's amazing after all these years, they don't even want to
remember you over here.

*Stan*

It is quite understandable why Laurel and Hardy were off to England, for this second tour of variety theatres. When their film career ended in 1945, the world's most popular film comedy duo were never again given a paid job in the USA. That's – NOTHING, nichts, nada, zero, zilch.

And despite their films being shown countless times on TV throughout the world, they never received one penny from them. On the one occasion they *were* invited into a studio to actually make a programme for TV, they still weren't paid.

As Hardy once said:

*"It's enough to make a man burst out crying."*

*"This is Your Life"* live broadcast – 1st December 1954

If it had not been for the Brits and Europeans rescuing these two fallen idols after they had been discarded, and giving them back their dignity as performers, thus enabling them to earn the money they needed to pay off horrendous debts, then the last years in the former film comedians' lives would have been a story of such tragedy that no fan would wish to even contemplate the vision.

So, after the 1952 British tour proved successful, Laurel and Hardy returned to Britain in October 1953, and did a third extended tour. But, sorry to say, our comedy heroes were not invited to play Europe/the Continent again.

In all, Laurel made visits to France in no less than five different years – 1927, 1932, 1947, 1950, and 1951, and Hardy had accompanied him on the latter four trips – all starting out from California. This is a remarkable statistic, especially when one considers that a huge percentage of Brits have never travelled to France. It is even more remarkable when one considers that, allegedly, less than fifty per cent of US citizens actually possess a passport.

Thought to be the last ever publicity shot taken of these two great friends and comedy partners, whose love and respect for each other as people and performers, was even stronger than the love between most brothers.

(Taken at the Hardy home, on or around 5th August 1956).

The five trips to Great Britain and Europe are also a surprising statistic as, up till the release of my books *LAUREL & HARDY – The British Tours*, and *LAUREL & HARDY – The US Tours*, the public and film fans' perception of Stan Laurel and Oliver Hardy was that the only travelling they ever did during their working partnership was to go, each and every day, from their respective homes to the studio – and back.

It was the love of the Europeans then which kept the comedy couple's career alive, and it is the present day love which still emanates from the countries they visited which is keeping their memories alive now, and so both the Boys and fans alike must be extremely grateful to have made the lasting bonds they secured when Laurel and Hardy made — The European Tours.

THE END
SLUT
HET EINDE
DAS ENDE
FINE
LE FIN

# LAUREL AND HARDY IN FUNLAND

Following, is a gallery of photos which could not be used on the text pages, but which deserve their place in the book.

**HATS ON!**

Performing their well-used "hat swap routine" for the cameras.

St. Lazare Rail Station, PARIS

(17th June 1950)

No hat swap here. Both Laurels, and both Hardys, looking dapper in their own hats.

Rail Station, MILAN — 24th June 1950

# AN AUDIENCE WITH LAUREL AND HARDY

It wasn't always the case that Stan and Babe were on stage whilst the audience looked on. During the European tours there were a number of occasions where THEY were the on-lookers.

The man with the programme up to his chin seems to be thinking:

"I know him. I've seen him somewhere before. Now where was it?"

Stockholm Circus
(10th October 1947)

(magazine scan)

Here's an unusual one. Laurel and Hardy ARE in the audience, but they are there to watch – THEMSELVES.

Paris Studios Cinema, Billancourt. (29th January 1951)

In case you are still puzzled, they are there for a preview screening of *Atoll K*.

## GIVE US A BREAK

As soon as they have finished their cigarette break, the two visiting VIPs
have to use their vacant digits to hold a pen, and sign autographs.

[Thought to have been taken at a press conference in Liège, first week in January 1948. Venue not known.]

## FACE TO FACE

Babe and Stan admiring caricatures of themselves bearing their Danish names: "Gokke ok Gøg." These were presented at the Banquet held in their honour at the Palace Hotel, Copenhagen.

1st October 1947

They were made with eye-holes so they could be worn as a mask.

If there is one thing stranger than having a 2-D mask of yourself —
it's having a 3-D mask of yourself.

# DRESSED FOR THE OCCASION

ABOVE: An informal appearance with the public at large.

BELOW: A formal appearance with the penguin pack.

(Unknown venue and occasion.)

## ME AND MY PAL

Ollie sharing a: "Have you heard this one … ?" moment.

Palace Hotel, Copenhagen.

1st October 1947

During a break in filming, at the Paris Studios, a couple of interlopers are spotted, at right.
Maybe Lucille was after her job back as a script and continuity girl,
which is the job she was doing when she and Babe first met.

[Photo with thanks to Paul E. Guierucki]

116

## PLAYING WITH THE BIG BOYS

Stan and Babe auditioning stand-ins for
Hardy, for the forthcoming film *Atoll K*.
The man holding Laurel aloft is
Victor Decottignies, who got the job.

PARIS

20th July 1950

## HELLO! BIG BOY

Suzy Delair bringing out Babe's feminine side at her News Year's Eve birthday party.
(Tour d'Argent, Paris — 31st December 1950)

# GETTING AROUND

Trains and planes are the usual form of long-distance transport, but for short distances Laurel and Hardy employed:

## CARS
### CARRIAGES
#### and COPTERS

**Leaving Rome station**

**Leaving Copenhagen Station**

**Leaving the ground**

Taken on the Cote d'Azur during a break in filming *Atoll K*. September 1950

118

## MYSTERY CASES

Throughout the 1947–48 British and European Tours, Laurel and Hardy travelled with forty pieces of luggage. Many of these had luggage labels on them from the places they had visited and the hotels they stayed at. (Hence the design on the cover of this book).

Below is a film still from the 1939 film *The Flying Deuces*, on which such luggage labels have also been stuck. These are as follows:
Both cases have a label from "HOTEL de LOUVRE, MARSEILLES."
Hardy's also has: "FRENCH LINE" and "PANAMA MAIL S.S. Co.", while Laurel's has: "METROPOLE HOTEL, BRUXELLES" and "PARK HOTEL, CARDIFF".

Now here is the mystery: Hardy didn't sail on the French Line until June 1950 (the *Caronia*). Stan and Babe didn't go to Marseilles until August 1950. They didn't stay at the Metropole Hotel, Bruxelles (Brussels) until December 1947, and they didn't stay at the Park Hotel, Cardiff (Wales) until September 1952. And it was June 1954 when they sailed through the Panama Canal together. So how come all those stickers were on their cases in 1939?
[AJM: If your theory is that someone in the prop department stuck them on, then he would have had to have been the greatest clairvoyant ever.]

## LOVE OF THE LOVED

Stan and Ollie had a great love of children, and always went out of their way to make their day.

But the greatest love of all was between each other,
which is what made their partnership, AND films, so great.

## LAUREL & HARDY – The British Tours (1st Edition)

This engaging book is the story of the love which the British public retained for these two comic legends after Hollywood had turned its back on them, and how they adapted from film- to stage-work, and survived through the changing *modes* of comedy, and the changing *moods* of theatre audiences.

Readers are given a full account of every theatre engagement and every act they worked with; their travel arrangements; the hotels they stayed in; the people they met; plus previously undocumented public appearances. Show business celebrities and acts from the Laurel and Hardy shows give anecdotes about these two most revered of comedians.

The 1932 city tour of England and Scotland is also featured, when crowds of thousands mobbed Laurel and Hardy and left them reeling from the onslaught.

First Edition. 320 pages. 100 illustrations — Hardback — 246mm x 189mm

(10 digit) ISBN 0-9521308-0-7 — (13 digit) ISBN 978-0-9521308-0-2

-----0-----

## LAUREL and HARDY – The U.S. Tours

After the two comedians meet at the Hal Roach Studios, the story diverts from the making of their films, and leads us into a parallel world of public appearances, show business events, theatre tours, wartime fund-raising tours, and troop shows.

Revealed for the first time ever are scores of previously unknown appearances: including numerous trips from the West to the East coast; three 'junkets' to Mexico; three major U.S. city-to-city stage tours; and even a tour of Caribbean islands. On the journey, the Boys meet a whole constellation of Hollywood stars; befriend a future President; and are invited to the Whitehouse. Readers will be captivated by the journey.

First Edition. 432 pages. Over 220 illustrations.

Paperback – 210 x 150mm (A5) – (ISBN 978-0-9521308-2-6)

-----0-----

## LAUREL and HARDY – The European Tours

"The European Tours" details not only the 1947-48 stage tours Laurel and Hardy played around Denmark, Sweden, France, and Belgium, but the year the two Hollywood comedians spent in France, during the making of their 1950-51 film *Atoll K*. Included in this is a promotional visit to Italy; plus details of two earlier visits to France — one by Laurel in 1927, and one by both comedians in 1932.

Readers will get to see the real men behind the screen characters of "Stan and Ollie" — how they coped with being mobbed everywhere they went; the exhaustion of a life of touring; and how they both worked on through serious illness to complete their last film.

From it all, Stan Laurel and Oliver Hardy emerge as lovable, but vulnerable, men – and readers will experience their every emotion throughout these previously undocumented tours.

Revised. 128 pages – 200 illustrations. Paperback – A4 – (ISBN 978-0-9521308-4-0)

-----0-----

## CHAPLIN – Stage by Stage

Contains every known stage appearance Chaplin made in the UK and, for the first time ever, the ones he made in Vaudeville, touring America with the Fred Karno Company of Comedians.

Along the way, many myths and mistakes from other works on Chaplin will be corrected, and many lies and legends exposed. But, in destroying the negative, a positive picture is built up of the very medium which created the man and the screen character "Chaplin."

Included are extracts from the scripts of the plays and sketches in which Chaplin appeared, complemented by contemporary reviews and plot descriptions, all of which help to complete the picture of the influences which affected Chaplin's later film work.

[Although it is a companion to "LAUREL – Stage by Stage" it contains far more text relating to Chaplin, plus numerous different and previously unpublished photos of him.]

Read and be Amazed!

First Edition. 258 pages – 130 illustrations. Paperback – A4 – (ISBN 978-0-9521308-1-9)

"Chaplin Stage by Stage" *provides a unique and indispensable record of Chaplin's career on the British stage and music hall and in American vaudeville in the formative fifteen years before he entered films. Marriot's phenomenal research gives us an exhaustive chronicle of Charlie's stage appearances – in addition to those of his father and his brother Sydney.* — [DAVID ROBINSON – Chaplin biographer.]

-----0-----

## LAUREL – Stage by Stage

"LAUREL - Stage by Stage" is the prequel to 'A.J' Marriot's previous books detailing Laurel and Hardy's "British Tours"– "US Tours," and "European Tours," and is a companion to "CHAPLIN – Stage by Stage."

It narrates for the first-time-ever all of Stan Laurel's stage shows, from his earliest appearances in British pantomime (as the teenage Stanley Jefferson), right up to his last-ever stage show before entering films.

Along the way he spends over three years touring with Charlie Chaplin, in the most-famous of all comedy troupes – the Fred Karno Company.

The next eight years are spent touring in U.S. vaudeville, playing in song-dance-and-comedy sketch acts with various partners.

Readers will experience every low and high as this comic genius tries to unshackle himself from the hardship and tedium of vaudeville, during a number of attempts to get into the world of film comedy. The amount of detail revealed about these "lost" tours is astounding.

First Edition. 272 pages – 200 illustrations. Paperback – A4 – (ISBN 978-0-9521308-5-7)

-----0-----

The many celebrities who have bought previous books written by "A.J" Marriot range from among Britain's best-loved British comedians; TV, film, and stage actors; and rock and pop stars, to some of Hollywood's most famous film directors and actors. Have you bought your copies yet?

To purchase, go to the website: www.laurelandhardybooks.com

OR e-mail: ajmarriot@aol.com for further details:

Lightning Source UK Ltd.
Milton Keynes UK
UKHW051119070422
401231UK00007B/351